my **revision** notes

OCR A2
CRIMINAL
LAW AND
THE SPECIAL
STUDY PAPER

Sue Teal
Craig Beauman

HODDER
EDUCATION

Orders:

please contact Bookpoint Ltd, 130 Milton Park, Abingdon, Oxon OX14 4SB.

Telephone: (44) 01235 827720.

Fax: (44) 01235 400454.

Lines are open from 9.00–5.00, Monday to Saturday, with a 24 hour message answering service. You can also order through our website www.hoddereducation.co.uk.

British Library Cataloguing in Publication Data

A catalogue record for this title is available from the British Library

ISBN: 9781444180558

First Published 2013
Impression number   10 9 8 7 6 5 4 3 2
Year   2016 2015 2014

Copyright © Sue Teal and Craig Beauman, 2013

Hachette UK's policy is to use papers that are natural, renewable and recyclable products and made from wood grown in sustainable forests. The logging and manufacturing processes are expected to conform to the environmental regulations of the country of origin.

Cover photo © Tolga TEZCAN/iStockphoto

Typeset by Datapage (India) Pvt. Ltd.

Printed in India for Hodder Education, an Hachette UK company, 338 Euston Road, London NW1 3BH.

Get the most from this book

Everyone has to decide his or her own revision strategy, but it is essential to review your work, learn it and test your understanding. These Revision Notes will help you to do that in a planned way, topic by topic. Use this book as the cornerstone of your revision and don't hesitate to write in it – personalise your notes and check your progress by ticking off each section as you revise.

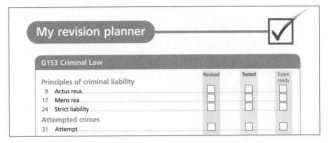

● practised the exam questions and gone online to check your answers.

✓ Tick to track your progress

Use the revision planner on pages 4 and 5 to plan your revision, topic by topic. Tick each box when you have:

● revised and understood a topic

● tested yourself

You can also keep track of your revision by ticking off each topic heading in the book. You may find it helpful to add your own notes as you work through each topic.

Features to help you succeed

Exam tips, summaries and comments

Throughout the book there are tips to help you boost your final grade.

Summaries provide advice on how to approach each topic in the exams.

Comments analyse student responses to exam questions, explaining why a student response will recieve a certain grade.

Typical mistakes

Examples of typical mistakes candidates make and how you can avoid them.

Key terms

Clear, concise definitions of essential key terms are provided on the page where they appear.

Exam practice

Practice exam questions are provided for each topic. Use them to consolidate your revision and practise your exam skills.

Now test yourself

These short, knowledge-based questions provide the first step in testing your learning. Answers are at the back of the book.

Student Activity

Use these questions to improve your knowledge and understanding.

Striving for an A/A*?

These useful tips will help you to answer exam questions well so that you can aim for better grades.

Online

Go online to check your answers to the exam practice questions at **www.therevisionbutton. co.uk/myrevisionnotes**

Check your understanding

Use the questions that have been set at the end of the topic to make sure that you understand each topic. Answers are at the back of the book.

Points for an essay

These are points that have been identified to help structure or improve an essay on each topic.

My revision planner

Countdown to my exams

6–8 weeks to go

- Start by looking at the specification – make sure you know exactly what material you need to revise and the style of the examination. Use the revision planner on pages 4 and 5 to familiarise yourself with the topics.
- Organise your notes, making sure you have covered everything on the specification. The revision planner will help you to group your notes into topics.
- Work out a realistic revision plan that will allow you time for relaxation. Set aside days and times for all the subjects that you need to study, and stick to your timetable.
- Set yourself sensible targets. Break your revision down into focused sessions of around 40 minutes, divided by breaks. These Revision Notes organise the basic facts into short, memorable sections to make revising easier.

Revised ☐

4–6 weeks to go

- Read through the relevant sections of this book and refer to the exam tips, exam summaries, typical mistakes and key terms. Tick off the topics as you feel confident about them. Highlight those topics you find difficult and look at them again in detail.
- Test your understanding of each topic by working through the 'Now test yourself' and 'Check your understanding' questions in the book. Look up the answers at the back of the book.
- Make a note of any problem areas as you revise, and ask your teacher to go over these in class.
- Look at past papers. They are one of the best ways to revise and practise your exam skills. Write or prepare planned answers to the exam practice questions provided in this book. Check your answers online at **www.therevisionbutton. co.uk/myrevisionnotes**
- Try different revision methods. For example, you can make notes using mind maps, spider diagrams or flash cards.
- Track your progress using the revision planner and give yourself a reward when you have achieved your target.

Revised ☐

One week to go

- Try to fit in at least one more timed practice of an entire past paper and seek feedback from your teacher, comparing your work closely with the mark scheme.
- Check the revision planner to make sure you haven't missed out any topics. Brush up on any areas of difficulty by talking them over with a friend or getting help from your teacher.
- Attend any revision classes put on by your teacher. Remember, he or she is an expert at preparing people for examinations.

Revised ☐

The day before the examination

- Flick through these Revision Notes for useful reminders, for example the exam tips, exam summaries, typical mistakes and key terms.
- Check the time and place of your examination.
- Make sure you have everything you need – extra pens and pencils, tissues, a watch, bottled water, sweets.
- Allow some time to relax and have an early night to ensure you are fresh and alert for the examination.

Revised ☐

My exams

A2 Criminal Law G153

Date: ....

Time: ....

Location: ....

A2 Criminal Law Special Study G154

Date: ....

Time: ....

Location: ....

G153 Criminal Law

How to use this section

- This section takes you through topics step by step.
- The list of cases is not exhaustive – it is fine to use other examples.
- This section provides ideas for AO2 points in essays – be sure that you can explain points clearly in your own words.
- Be active in your revision.
- Know what works well for you.
- Use colours, images and even sounds in your revision – anything which will trigger your memory in an exam situation.
- Practise working to time limits.
- Look at the sample exam practice answers online at **www.therevisionbutton.co.uk/myrevisionnotes**

Know your exam – G153

- 2-hour paper worth 120 marks.
- Eight questions.
- Section A – essay question worth 50 marks – one question from a choice of three.
- Section B – hypothetical problem question/case study worth 50 marks – one question from a choice of three.
- Section C – objective reasoning question worth 20 marks – one question from a choice of two.

Make the best of what you have

- Read all the questions before you start.
- Plan your answer before writing.
- Have a wide base of knowledge but focus on the law rather than facts.
- Practise linking cases to principles and analysis.
- Consider AO2 points beforehand and try to get beyond the obvious.
- Do as the question asks.
- Use your time wisely – resist the temptation to spend too long on any one question.
- Consider doing questions in a different order, for example, you could do Section C first (as this may take you less than the notionally allotted 30 minutes and allows you to plan better for the remaining questions), followed by Section B (you are still in problem-solving mode) and finally Section A (you know exactly how much time remains and if you are short of time you can make notes on a topic you know well rather than trying to solve a hypothetical problem question when you are under pressure).
- Take care with your presentation.

Section A – How to do well

- Answer the question you have been asked and make a plan.
- Have an introduction to show that you have engaged with the question.
- Make sure your knowledge is accurate and wide-ranging – this includes definitions, cases and any relevant statute law.
- Focus on the law rather than the facts.
- Use factual material in a way that makes sense, perhaps through development over time.

- Make comment and analysis throughout your answer rather than in a single block towards the end of the essay.
- Try to do more than simply repeating command words from the question.
- Reach a conclusion relevant to the title.

Section B – How to do well

- Read the scenario carefully and highlight key material.
- Plan before you start to write.
- Begin by identifying relevant areas of law, including offences and defences.
- Make sure that you give clear and accurate definitions of law and legal principle.
- Support this with accurate use of cases and statute law.
- Apply the law to the facts in the scenario.
- Reach a conclusion if at all possible.
- Be methodical and consider offences or characters one at a time.
- Consider and apply any relevant defences.

Section C – How to do well

- Read all the statements carefully.
- Plan your answers.
- Reason logically – writing in bullet points can be helpful.
- Apply the law and use the facts in the scenario.
- Be concise and do not use cases.
- Be decisive.
- End with a conclusion to the statement.

Other things to help you

- Look at past papers, mark schemes and examiner reports – your teacher may give these to you but you can also read them for yourself at **http://www.ocr.org.uk/qualifications/as-a-level-gce-law-h134-h534/** and follow the links.

1 Actus reus

This chapter relates to two key areas:

- omissions
- causation.

What is an actus reus in law?

Revised

- The conduct element.
- Can be a positive act.
- Can be an omission when there is a duty to act.
- Sometimes it is simply 'being there'.

Why is there a law on actus reus?

Revised

- Innocent people are harmed in different ways.
- To protect, liability must be drawn flexibly.
- It is normally accompanied by an appropriate *mens rea* so criminal law is built on fault.

The different aspects of actus reus

Revised

Need for a voluntary act

- Defendant must have control over what they do or fail to do.
- Can be hard to decide when this line is crossed.

Being there/state of affairs

- Simply being in the wrong place at the wrong time.
- Can seem very unjust and is rare.

Examples

Larsonneur (1933): L was told to leave the UK. She left but was deported back to the UK. She was arrested, charged with being 'an alien' and convicted.

Winzar (1983): W was taken to hospital, but when found to be simply drunk, was told to leave. W was found in a corridor, the police were called and they sat W on the side of the road. W was convicted of being drunk on the highway.

Result of actus reus

- Liability is determined by the consequence the *actus reus* leads to.
- Can be hard to decide on the most appropriate charge.

Omissions

Definition

- A failure to act creates criminal liability.
- A duty situation must exist.

Statutory duty

- Created by Parliament looking after society – known as 'social paternalism'. Examples include:
  - s6 Road Traffic Act 1984
  - s170 Road Traffic Act 1984
  - s1 Children and Young Persons Act 1933
  - s5 Domestic Violence, Crime and Victims Act 2004.

Contractual duty

- A job of work creates liability, for example a teacher or lifeguard.

Duty created by official position

- Specific extension of contractual duty – for example the police.

Duty created by relationship

- Often an accepted relationship, such as between parent and child.

Voluntary assumption of a duty based on reliance

- A person takes on the duty to care for another.

Creation of a dangerous situation leading to a duty

- A person starts a series of events and their failure to act leads to harm.

> **Exam tip**
>
> **Section A** – be thorough in your knowledge of duty categories and use relevant case examples. Develop AO2 by considering the reasons behind each duty, and its limits.
>
> **Section B** – a good grasp of relevant cases will help you spot duty situations in a scenario.

> **Typical mistake**
>
> **Section A** – striking the wrong balance by spending too much time on factual intricacies. Only 25 marks of a potential 50 are awarded for AO1 so usually a brief and accurate synopsis is enough.
>
> **Section B** and **Section C** – lack of planning can make an answer confused and rambling.

Key cases on omissions

Case name	Factual trigger	Type of duty	Legal point
Pittwood (1902)	P failed to set railway crossing, leading to death	Contract	P convicted of manslaughter as did not do job contracted to do
Adomako (1995)	A, an anaesthetist, failed to spot important tube disconnected during operation, which led to patient's death	Contract	A convicted of manslaughter as behaved in way far below what could be expected of someone in that position
Dytham (1979)	D, a police officer on duty, saw fight but went off duty without reporting fight or alerting other officers	Official position	D convicted of misconduct in public office as could have done something
Gibbins and Proctor (1918)	G, father of a seven-year-old girl, lived with P. Isolated child and deliberately starved her to death	Relationship Assumption of duty based on reliance	G convicted of murder based on his relationship P convicted of murder as she assumed duty to care for child
Instan (1893)	I moved in with elderly aunt as carer but when aunt became ill I ignored her and ate food. Aunt died	Assumption of duty based on reliance	I convicted of manslaughter as had volunteered to care for aunt
Stone and Dobinson (1977)	S's eccentric sister, who had an eating disorder, came to live with S and D. They tried to help but were ineffectual and sister died	Assumption of duty based on reliance	S and D were convicted of manslaughter even though they could not do more because they assumed a duty of care for F

(Continued)

(Continued)

Case name	Factual trigger	Type of duty	Legal point
Miller (1983)	M, a squatter smoking in bed, set mattress alight and went to another room, leaving fire to get worse	Duty through creation of dangerous situation	M convicted of arson as could have done something after realising the situation he had created
Santana-Bermudez (2003)	S asked if anything sharp in pocket before being searched by policewoman. He said not but policewoman scratched by needle in S's pocket	Duty through creation of dangerous situation	S convicted under s47 OAPA 1861 as could have told truth
Evans (2009)	E bought and gave heroin to half-sister, who self-injected heroin. Girl collapsed so E and mother put her to bed, hoping she would recover, but she died	Duty through creation of dangerous situation	Mother and E convicted of manslaughter as created situation in which girl died

Limit of a duty

- A person of sound mind can release another from their duty to care.

- Sometimes a duty can change and end.

- A duty may not exist in the first place.

Key cases on limit of a duty

Case name	Factual trigger	Limit of duty	Legal point
Smith (1979)	S's wife was so scared of doctors she would not allow S to get doctor when baby stillborn. When S did get doctor wife so ill she died	Release from duty	S charged with manslaughter but not convicted
Re B (2002)	B held competent to make own decision about discontinuation of life-preserving treatment	Release from duty	Those providing treatment released from duty
Bland (1993)	B in persistent vegetative state. After three years, it was clear B would not recover and application made to stop treatment	End of duty	Duty to care replaced by duty to act in B's best interests, so failure to continue treating not criminal
Khan and Khan (1998)	K and K were drug dealers who gave heroin to girl who self-injected. She collapsed, K and K left, and the girl died	No duty in existence	K and K manslaughter convictions quashed as CA said no duty situation between drug dealers and victim

Reform proposals for omissions

- Law Commission Draft Criminal Code 1989:
  - Clause 17 – liability for omission when there is a duty to act.
  - Clause 23 – liability for creating a dangerous situation and not doing what is reasonable to stop it occurring or continuing.
- Creation of a common duty to act – this would need to be carefully framed.

Points for an essay on omissions

- Terminology:
  - 1989 Law Commission Draft Criminal Code preferred 'external element'.
- Breadth of liability:
  - Not always easy to decide if a duty exists.
  - Decisions often made on a case-by-case basis, causing uncertainty.
  - Law can expand when necessary – for example, to deal with drug dealers and the consequences of drugs they supply.
  - Arguably unfair that a person owing a duty who does nothing can be liable, while a stranger who watches something horrific and does nothing is not liable.
- Is automatic liability once a duty is assumed fair?
  - Arguably a person should accept responsibility for a duty they assume.
  - However, they may not know its full extent or be able to see it through.

- Protection offered to doctors:
  - Essential so doctors are not in constant fear of litigation.
  - Doctors may be over-protected as they have to behave very badly to be liable.
  - Some judicial flexibility to say a duty to act in the patient's best interests prevails over a duty to treat.
  - Issues surrounding euthanasia continue.
- Ending of a duty:
  - Arguably a mentally competent adult should be able to make their own decisions, even those that lead to death.
  - A duty may arise where a person is vulnerable and needs protecting but a small act, such as summoning help, may be enough.
  - Emotional cases are hard for juries.
- Good Samaritan law:
  - Exists elsewhere, such as France, and is based on commonly accepted moral principles.
  - Makes people take responsibility for their actions but potentially extends duties even to strangers.
  - People may be put in situations they are not competent to deal with.
  - Limits become hard to define.
  - Must someone put themselves at risk to help another?
  - What happens when many people appear to have a duty to act?
- Complexity for Parliament:
  - Social paternalism allows duties to be created and extended for society's protection, encouraging people to be good citizens.
  - Legislation does not necessarily improve behaviour – photographers in Princess Diana case.
  - Could lead to the creation of a new offence, as in Holland, of a failure to rescue.

Check your understanding

1. Name three examples of an *actus reus*.
2. Give an example of a statute which creates liability for an omission.
3. Explain the difference between a contractual duty and one resulting from an official position.
4. Explain whether the law is fair in creating liability based on the assumption of a duty to care.
5. Explain three problems associated with the creation of a Good Samaritan law.

Now test yourself

Tested

1. Look at the chart and note down the reason why there is a duty in each case.

Tip: some cases are covered by more than one duty.

Case	Duty
Pittwood (1902)	
Dytham (1979)	
Instan (1893)	
Gibbins and Proctor (1918)	
Stone and Dobinson (1977)	
Evans (2009)	
Miller (1983)	
Santana-Bermudez (2003)	
Adomako (1995)	

2. Copy the table below and then fill in the details to test your knowledge and then make a revision chart with the cases grouped appropriately.

Case name	Factual key words	Area of causation	Legal importance
Evans (2009)			
Khan and Khan (1998)			
Pittwood (1902)			
Instan (1983)			
Re B (2002)			
Adomako (1995)			
Gibbins and Proctor (1918)			
Smith (1979)			
Bland (1993)			
Stone and Dobinson (1977)			
Dytham (1979)			
Santana-Bermudez (2003)			
Miller (1983)			

Causation

Revised

Causation in fact

- Consequence occurs because of the defendant's conduct – 'but for' test.

Causation in law

- Defendant must be a more-than-minimal cause of the harm – *de minimis* principle – a 'more than slight or trifling link'.

Chain of causation – a novus actus interveniens (NAI)

- Must link defendant's conduct to the result.
- Can be broken by a new, intervening act, independent of the defendant.
- Must be serious enough to break the chain.

Cause 1: What the victim does

- 'Fight or flight'.
- Acting in a foreseeable way does not break the chain – 'daftness' test.
- Acting in an unforeseeable way may break the chain.
- Defendant must take their victim as they find them – 'thin skull' rule.
- Self-neglect does not break the chain even if a refusal to be treated is extreme.
- Deliberate voluntary acts of the victim can break the chain.

Cause 2: What a third party does

- If the defendant's conduct leads the victim to do something foreseeable the chain of causation usually remains intact.

Cause 3: An event which is natural but unpredictable

- Medical treatment rarely breaks the chain of causation, unless so independent of the defendant's conduct and making it insignificant in causing death.
- Turning off a life-support machine will not break the chain of causation.

Key cases on causation

Case name	Summary facts	Causation element	Legal point
White (1910)	Poison in mother's drink	Fact – but for	W not liable for murder as mother did not die 'but for' W's act
Roberts (1972)	R picked up female hitchhiker who jumped out of car, thinking R going to grab her	Fact – but for NAI – daftness	R 'but for' cause of injuries and convicted under s47 OAPA 1861
Kimsey (1996)	K lost control in high speed car chase, killing other driver	Law – de minimis	K's act sufficient cause, although not sole cause as other driver also speeding
Smith (1959)	S stabbed fellow soldier who was dropped when taken for medical help. Treatment made injury worse, leading to death	Law – operative and substantial NAI – medical treatment	S liable for murder as stab wound operational and substantial, if not only cause, of death
Marjoram (2000)	M in group shouting abuse and kicking hostel door. As door kicked open, victim fell or jumped out of window and was badly hurt	NAI – foreseeable act by victim	M convicted under s20 OAPA 1861 as victim's reaction foreseeable
Corbett (1996)	C punched and head-butted man who ran off, tripped and fell into road, where killed by car	NAI – daftness and foreseeable act by victim	C's manslaughter conviction upheld by CA as victim not overreacted or been 'daft'
Williams (1992)	W and others picked up hitchhiker who jumped out of car at 30 mph and died	NAI – daftness and foreseeable act by victim	W's manslaughter conviction quashed by CA as victim's act not foreseeable and disproportionate
Blaue (1975)	B stabbed Jehovah's Witness, who refused life-saving blood transfusion and died	NAI – thin skull	B guilty of murder as had to take victim as found
Holland (1841)	H deliberately cut man's finger. Cut became infected and man told amputation necessary but he delayed and died of blood poisoning	NAI – self-neglect	H liable for man's death even though victim's behaviour extreme
Dear (1996)	D attacked man with knife. Victim did not get treatment and possibly made injury worse. Victim died from loss of blood	NAI – self-neglect	D liable even though victim probably made things worse
Kennedy (2007)	K gave syringe of heroin to man who self-injected and died	NAI – victim's own deliberate act	K's manslaughter conviction quashed based on free-will to self-inject
Benge (1865)	B was in charge of railway workers and misread timetable so workers on track. Although he tried to alert driver, several people killed	NAI – third party act	Several factors led to deaths, not least driver failure, but B convicted as main cause
Pagett (1983)	P used pregnant girlfriend as human shield. Police returned P's fire and girl killed	NAI – third party act	Although police trained to use guns foreseeable would return P's fire

(Continued)

(Continued)

Case name	Summary facts	Causation element	Legal point
Cheshire (1991)	C shot man who needed surgery and tracheotomy. Two months later victim died of tracheotomy complications	NAI – medical treatment	C liable as acts contributed significantly to death
Jordan (1956)	J stabbed man who almost recovered but doctor gave antibiotic without checking and victim died	NAI – medical treatment	J not liable as doctor's conduct 'palpably wrong'
Malcherek (1981)	M's victim on life-support machine and machine turned off	NAI – medical treatment	M's murder conviction upheld as CA said 'bizarre' that turning off machine could break chain

Points for an essay on omissions

- Causation in fact is simple and effective.
- It is justifiable as a natural basis for liability.
- It fits the concept of personal responsibility.
- However, it always goes back to the original actor which might be unjust.
- Causation in law is often hard to prove and policy considerations can override legal principles.
- Other factors such as 'thin skull' can cloud the issue: is conviction fair when something is completely invisible or unpredictably severe?
- That a chain of causation exists is often hard to define and may be stretched to facilitate conviction.
- Policy factors with regard to the police and doctors are essential so they can do their job but can appear to be generous and not provide justice for victims and their families.

Check your understanding

6. Why is the case of *Jordan* (1956) of particular importance?
7. Give three situations in which the chain of causation may be broken.
8. How does the 'but for' test work and what is good and bad about this test?
9. What is the significance of *Kennedy* (2007) and why was this case so difficult for the judges?
10. In one sentence, explain why the 'thin skull' test is useful. In one sentence, explain why the test is problematic.

Now test yourself

Tested ☐

3. Copy the table below and then fill in the details to test your knowledge and then make a revision chart with the cases grouped appropriately.

Case name	Factual key words	Area of causation	Legal importance
Jordan (1956)			
Kimsey (1996)			
Williams (1992)			
Pagett (1983)			
Smith (1959)			
White (1910)			
Blaue (1975)			

(Continued)

(Continued)

Case name	Factual key words	Area of causation	Legal importance
Cheshire (1991)			
Dear (1996)			
Roberts (1972)			
Malcherek (1981)			
Corbett (1996)			
Kennedy (2007)			
Marjoram (2000)			
Holland (1841)			
Benge (1865)			

Exam summary

✔ This topic is relevant in all areas of the exam paper.

✔ **Section A** – essays usually focus on either causation or omissions. There is plenty of AO2 and development helps you reach the higher mark bands. Good case reference is vital; focus on the legal point as a few key words on the facts will usually suffice. Fewer cases used well is better than extensive citation with little or no amplification. Do not over-write even though this might be a topic you really enjoy.

✔ **Section B** and **Section C** – *actus reus* is likely to be one element among several to be considered. Read the question carefully to make sure you are giving the correct information and then define, explain and apply accurately and confidently.

Striving for an A/A*?

1. Ensure knowledge is sound, confident and well organised.
2. Take your research further – for example, read what the Law Commission has had to say – **http://www.bailii. org/ew/other/EWLC/1989/177_1.pdf**.
3. **Section A** – practise developing analytical points but be flexible and respond to the question.
4. **Section B** – read the question carefully to strike the right balance.
5. **Section C** – apply principles concisely and logically.

2 Mens rea

This chapter relates primarily to two key areas:

- intention
- recklessness.

Other issues are:
- negligence
- knowledge
- transferred malice
- coincidence.

Exam tip

Section A – the development of the law through the cases is very important. You need to be able to explain the evolution of the law so your chronology must be clear. Changes in the test are often subtle so be precise in your explanations, commenting on the tests and their usefulness.

Section B and **Section C** – focus on explaining, and then applying, the current law.

What is mens rea in law?   Revised

- The mental element.
- A barometer of culpability that determines the level of responsibility and punishment.

Intention   Revised

Definition

- There must be an intention for a particular result.
- Intention relates to the defendant's aim, purpose or desire.

Motive

- Irrelevant when deciding on intention.

Typical mistake

This topic comprises a lot of cases and it is easy to have an overly factual bias. To reach the higher mark bands it is vital to be clear and accurate on the law, its development through the cases and its problems.

Example

Steane (1947): S made war-time propaganda broadcasts and said he did so because of threats to himself and his family. It was held that his intention was the key and not his motives for acting.

Direct intent

- Defendant sets out to make the prohibited consequence occur.
- This is an easier *mens rea* to prove although it is quite rare.

Oblique intent/foresight of consequences

- Defendant does not necessarily intend an outcome to occur but realises that it is almost inevitable – this is virtual certainty.
- Concept largely developed by judges.
- Initially assessed objectively.
- Some Parliamentary guidance in s8 Criminal Justice Act 1967 and test is now subjective.
- Evolution of test is complex.

Key cases and statute law on intention

Case	Facts	Test	Problem
DPP v Smith (1961)	Killed policeman with car	Objective test applied – standard of reasonable man	Does not consider blameworthiness of defendant
Criminal Justice Act 1967		s8 – foresight assessed subjectively and all evidence taken into account. Jury not bound to infer intent simply based on consequence being natural and probable	
Hyam (1985)	Letterbox petrol bomb causes death	HL – intention to kill or cause GBH as likely or highly likely consequence sufficient. Lord Hailsham dissented and clear s8 must be followed	51 per cent probability enough for murder – is this too low?
Moloney (1985)	Drunken duel causes death	HL – Lord Bridge – was death or really serious injury natural and probable consequence and did defendant see it as such?	What is natural consequence? No mention of probability
Hancock and Shankland (1986)	Striking miners on motorway bridge	HL – Lord Scarman – greater probability of consequence more likely was foreseen and more probable that intended	Used probability without quantifying amount
Nedrick (1986)	Letterbox petrol bomb causes death	CA – Lord Lane – consequence to be virtual certainty and defendant to realise this – evidence from which jury could infer intention	Clarification of virtual certainty test but only CA decision
Woollin (1998)	Baby thrown towards pram and dies	HL – Lord Steyn – virtual certainty test to be used – if satisfied, jury find intention	Endorses virtual certainty but changes 'infer' to 'find'
Re A (2000)	Conjoined twins, one twin dies	CA – followed Woollin and said foresight equalled intention	Civil Division case and therefore only persuasive precedent
Matthews and Alleyne (2003)	Man drowned after thrown off bridge	CA – direct intention or appreciation of death as virtual certainty means jury may infer intention but do not have to find it	Criminal Division case and not been tested in a higher court

The hardest part of intention

Example

Woollin (1998): the trial judge said the jury might infer intention if W had appreciated a substantial risk of harm or serious harm when he threw the baby. W was convicted and appealed, saying that the test of virtual certainty should have been used. The CA retained the murder conviction but in the HL the conviction was reduced to manslaughter. Lord Steyn laid down a model direction to the effect that a jury are not entitled to find intention unless they feel sure that death or serious bodily harm is a virtual certainty and the defendant appreciated that to be the case.

- As HL decision this is the leading case but it does not solve all the problems.
- Changes in judicial wording can be difficult to follow but a grasp of the main ideas of each case is essential in an essay.
- In a problem question the *Woollin* test is the one to apply.

Reform proposals for intention

Reform body	Reform proposal
Law Commission 1989	Draft Criminal Code – Clause 18(b) – a person acts intentionally with respect to (a) a circumstance when he hopes or knows that it exists or will exist; (b) a result when he acts either in order to bring it about or being aware that it will occur in the ordinary course of events.
Law Commission 1993	A person acts intentionally with respect to a result when it is his purpose to cause it, or although it is not his purpose to cause it, he knows that it would occur in the ordinary course of events if he were to succeed in his purpose of causing some other result.
Law Commission 2004	A person should be taken to intend a result if he or she acts in order to bring it about. In cases where the judge believes that justice may not be done unless an expanded understanding of intention is given, the jury should be directed as follows: an intention to bring about a result may be found if it is shown that the defendant thought that the result was a virtually certain consequence of his or her action.

Points for an essay on intention

- Source of test:
  - Developed by judges, so easy to say Parliament should intervene.
  - Planned in the Offences Against the Person Bill 1998, using the *Nedrick/Woollin* test, but not enacted.
  - Critics argue that problems could still remain.
  - *Woollin* is good as it clarifies the virtual certainty test but infer/find debate is unhelpful and ongoing.
- Nature of test:
  - Objective test flawed – blameworthiness should be assessed from the defendant's perspective.
  - Subjective test more credible – particularly important in murder due to mandatory life sentence.
- Words used:
  - Likely/highly likely – set the bar of liability too low and blurred the line between intention and recklessness and between murder and manslaughter.
  - Natural and probable – both words are vital as a natural consequence is not necessarily probable – a baby is a natural consequence of sex but in fact a highly improbable one.
  - Virtual certainty – simpler language and more easily quantifiable as meaning almost nothing else can happen, closer to at least 90 per cent probability.
  - Early tests were complex for jurors and judges, often leading to appeals, but a clearer test gives a better chance of the correct verdict.
- Academic criticisms of 1989 reform proposals – Professor Sir John Smith:
  - Phrase 'being aware' blurs intention and recklessness and the line between murder and manslaughter.
  - Phrase 'will occur' is overly restrictive and excludes situations that should be covered by intention.
  - A defendant might be deemed to have intended a consequence they tried to avoid.
- Motive:
  - Not taken into account.
  - Seems unfair when people have good motives, for example, euthanasia.

Check your understanding

1. Give a simple definition, and an example, of direct intention.
2. Give a simple definition, and an example, of oblique intention.
3. Why was s8 Criminal Justice Act 1967 so important?
4. What key word was omitted for the test in *Moloney (1985)* and why was it so important?
5. Why is the test created by *Nedrick (1986)* so helpful to jurors? Give a figure to quantify the level of foresight it requires.

Now test yourself

Tested ☐

1. How good is your knowledge? Intention is more difficult than it looks and knowledge must be clear, precise and well organised. Copy the table below, fill in the details, and then use it to make a revision mindmap of the cases on foresight of consequences. You can start with the oldest case first and work forwards or start with the current test and then show how the courts developed the law.

Case name	Summary facts	Test

(Continued)

(Continued)

Case name	Summary facts	Test

Recklessness

Revised

Definition

- Risk taking.
- Definition from 1989 Draft Criminal Code – a person acts recklessly with respect to (a) a circumstance when he is aware of a risk that it exists or will exist; (b) a result when he is aware of a risk that it will occur, and it is, in the circumstances known to him, unreasonable to take the risk.

Subjective recklessness

- Defendant sees the risk and decides to run it.

Objective recklessness

- Defendant did not see a risk which was obvious to the reasonable man.

Key cases on recklessness

Case name	Summary facts	Test
Cunningham (1957)	Gas meter pulled off a wall sending fumes into house next door	Subjective – C did not intend to cause harm and had not taken known risk
Caldwell (1982)	Fire in hotel	Objective – C said so drunk did not realise lives might be endangered but convicted as reasonable man would have seen risk
Elliot v C (1983)	Girl with learning difficulties set fire to shed	Objective – girl did not see risk, and could not see it, but convicted as reasonable man would have seen risk
G and another (2003)	Boys set wheelie bin on fire causing £1m damage	Objective – trial judge directed jury to consider whether reasonable man would have seen risk. Boys convicted Subjective – HL quashed conviction and overruled Caldwell
Lidar (2000)	Bouncer killed under wheels of L's car	Subjective – L convicted as saw highly probable risk of serious injury or death to bouncer hanging on to car and L took risk

The role of recklessness now

- Widely used, as intention is rarely required and can be hard to prove.
- Seen as a 'human' state of mind – we all take risks, although some more than others!
- Applies to a wide range of offences, from criminal damage to manslaughter.

Points for an essay on recklessness

- The subjective test – good for defendants:
  - Equates with blameworthiness by focusing on whether the defendant was at fault by seeing the risk and deciding to run it.
  - Encourages people to take responsibility and has a deterrent effect.
  - Avoids injustice when the defendant cannot see the risk.
  - Looks at the characteristics of the defendant when deciding whether they saw the risk and decided to take it.
- The subjective test – bad for victims:
  - Conviction relies on the defendant seeing the risk. This can leave many victims and families without the satisfaction of knowing that there has been a conviction.
  - Notoriously difficult to prove what a defendant was thinking.
  - Not a level playing field regarding blame and responsibility because the defendant's characteristics are less relevant.

Negligence

Revised

Definition

- Defendant falls so far short of the standards of the reasonable man as to create criminal liability.
- Objective test.

Use of negligence

- Driving offences, for example s3 Road Traffic Act 1988.
- Gross negligence manslaughter – see page 47.

Knowledge

Revised

Definition

- Defendant can be liable when they do something 'knowingly'.

Example

Sweet v Parsley (1969): the defendant owned a house which she let out. The tenants were smoking cannabis there but the defendant did not know that. She was convicted of 'being concerned in the management of premises used for the smoking of cannabis resin'. The HL overturned the conviction because she did not know cannabis was being smoked in the house.

Transferred malice

Definition

- Defendant intends something to happen to a person but it happens to someone else.

Examples

Latimer (1886): L meant to hit a man who had attacked him but the belt he was using bounced off the man and hit a woman. L was found guilty of an assault on the woman.

AG Ref (No 3 of 1994) (1997): a man attacked a pregnant woman whose baby died of the injuries suffered in the attack after it was born and the HL said that transferred malice was a valid principle of law.

Gnango (2012): G exchanged fire with another gunman and a girl neither gunmen was aiming at was shot and killed. The trial judge applied transferred malice. The CA allowed G's appeal, saying that 'joint enterprise' liability for murder could not arise on the facts but the Supreme Court restored G's murder conviction as he was a principal to an agreement to engage in unlawful violence specifically designed to cause death or serious injury.

Limit of liability

- If the defendant has *mens rea* for a totally different offence than the one which occurs there is no liability.

Example

Pembliton (1874): P threw a stone intending to hit people but broke a window instead. He was convicted but this was overturned on appeal.

Coincidence of actus reus and mens rea

Definition

- Point at which the *actus reus* and *mens rea* of the crime come together.
- May only be momentary.
- Whole sequence of events may be spread over a period of time.

Key cases on coincidence

Case name	Summary facts	Coincidence
Thabo Meli v R (1954)	T and others attacked man and threw him over cliff, thinking he was dead. Man died from exposure	Guilty – *actus reus* and *mens rea* came together even though man died later from cause not considered by defendants
Church (1966)	C threw woman into river believing her to be dead. Woman died of drowning	Guilty – *actus reus* and *mens rea* came together even though woman not dead when thrown into river
Fagan (1986)	F parked his car on policeman's foot	Guilty – there was *mens rea* for *actus reus* of applying force to policeman's foot when F turned ignition off
Le Brun (1991)	Woman died after being dropped by husband	Guilty – *actus reus* and *mens rea* came together in course of man and woman having argument, woman falling down, and being dropped by husband trying to pick her up while drunk

Check your understanding

6. Give a simple definition, and an example of, subjective recklessness.
7. Give a simple definition, and an example of, objective recklessness.
8. Name an offence for which negligence is a sufficient level of *mens rea*.
9. Explain what is meant by coincidence. Why is it an important theory in criminal law?
10. Why is transferred malice important?

Now test yourself

Tested ☐

2. For each of the following scenarios decide whether there is likely to be an offence, based on the existence of *mens rea*, and give a brief justification for your answer.

   a) Andy's girlfriend, Jan, has left him for another man. Andy calls Jan but she tells him their relationship is over. Andy is so upset he goes to Jan's house with a loaded gun, intending to threaten to kill himself if she will not take him back. Jan is in the garden and she starts to swear at Andy. Andy gets angry and waves the gun at Jan. He pulls the trigger and Jan is killed.

   b) Peter is a chef who has been sacked for being drunk at work. As he is leaving work with his things Peter puts a pan of oil on the stove with the heat turned up high. No one notices the pan and a fire starts, damaging the kitchen.

   c) Coral has an argument with her boyfriend, Frank. Coral pushes Frank and he trips, hitting his head. As Frank lies on the floor there is a lot of blood and Coral thinks he is dead. She runs off. A passerby calls an ambulance and Frank is taken to hospital as he is still alive. Frank dies an hour later.

   d) Clive is an animal rights activist and he decided to plant a bomb under the car of a scientist who does experiments on animals. The bomb explodes and kills the scientist's wife.

Exam tip

Section A – be sure to learn all elements of *mens rea* thoroughly. Practise combining factual and analytical material and be precise in explaining tests.

Section B – remember to give the current test for *mens rea* clearly and concisely and then apply it accurately. Negligence, knowledge, transferred malice and coincidence are also relevant as they link into other topics covered elsewhere in this guide.

Section C – *mens rea* is most likely to be one of the elements of an offence that needs to be proved.

Typical mistake

Don't fall into the trap of thinking that this topic is one about which you can write without solid revision – a lack of precision and clarity shows up all too easily!

Striving for an A/A*?

1. Practise getting intention cases in the right order.
2. Take your research further – for example, read the relevant section of the Draft Criminal Code (see Chapter 1).
3. **Section A** – analytical points on the development of the law, and its current state, are important.
4. **Section B** – concentrate on thorough, confident and clear application of relevant law to the facts given. Remember that *mens rea* is half of most offences.
5. **Section C** – apply principles logically and precisely.

3 Strict liability

This chapter relates to two key areas:

- absolute liability
- strict liability.

Exam tip

Section A – be clear on definitions, using the principles created by the *Gammon* test, and explore a wide range of AO2 issues.

Section B and **Section C** – be familiar with the principles which underlie strict liability and be aware that scenarios may well be based closely on decided cases.

Typical mistake

Try not to spend too much time on the factual content of cases as analysis is plentiful and you need to strike a good balance. You do not need to know details of the areas covered by strict liability – knowing the cases is sufficient.

What is the difference between strict and absolute liability?

Revised

- Strict liability – *mens rea* is not needed for at least one element of a voluntary *actus reus*.

Example

Pharmaceutical Society of GB v Storkwain (1986): S was charged with an offence under s58(2) Medicines Act 1968 of supplying drugs without a doctor's prescription. S supplied drugs for a prescription that was later discovered to be forged and was liable, even though there was no evidence of intention, recklessness or negligence.

- Absolute liability – no *mens rea* is required at all and the *actus reus* need not be voluntary.

Examples

Larsonneur (1933): L, who was French, was ordered to leave the UK but the country she went to deported her because she did not have the correct papers. L was found guilty of an offence under the Aliens Order 1920 as she had no leave to land in the UK and was found there.

Winzar v CC of Kent (1983): W was taken to hospital because he appeared ill. In fact he was drunk and was told to leave, but was found later on a chair in a corridor. The police took W to the road outside and he was convicted of being found drunk on a highway under s12 Licensing Act 1892.

Why does strict liability exist?

Revised

- To regulate behaviour.
- To drive up standards.
- To fill necessary gaps with offences that are easy to create – over 3500 exist.

What are the general principles of strict liability?

Revised

A lack of mens rea

- There is an initial presumption for *mens rea* but if it is not needed for at least one element of the *actus reus* the offence may be classed as strict liability.

No need for fault

- Defendant can be liable even if the prohibited consequence occurs inadvertently and their act was totally blameless.

No defence of 'all due diligence'

- *Everything within his power not to commit the offence.*
- Sometimes Parliament has incorporated a defence of due diligence.

- This is erratic and often illogical.

No defence of mistake

- No defence even if the mistake is honest.

- This runs counter to principles found elsewhere in criminal law.

Key cases on general principles

Case	Summary facts	Area of strict liability	Point of law in case
Prince (1875)	P took girl from her father, reasonably believing her to be 18 or over. She was under 18	No need for *mens rea* for all aspects of offence	P intended to take girl and liability strict as to age to protect young girls
Hibbert (1869)	H met a girl aged 14 and they had sex	No need for *mens rea* for all aspects of offence	H not convicted as no proof he intended to remove girl from her father even though liability strict as to her age
Callow v Tillstone (1900)	Butcher convicted of exposing unsound meat for sale	No need for fault	Irrelevant that vet passed meat as fit for human consumption
Harrow LBC v Shah and Shah (1999)	Employee sold lottery ticket to child aged 13, mistakenly thinking over 16	No due diligence	Conviction even though given employees instructions on checking for age before sale and nothing more could have been done
Cundy v Le Cocq (1884)	Defendant charged with selling intoxicating liquor to drunken person	No mistake	Sale proved to have taken place and drunken state could have been observed, even though no obvious evidence of it
Sherras v De Rutzen (1895)	Defendant's daughter sold alcohol to constable on duty, but no way of knowing due to lack of police armband	No mistake	Conviction quashed as nothing defendant could do to prevent offence

Is strict liability always statutory?

Revised

- Most offences created by Parliament but a few remain in common law.

Example

Gibson and Sylverie (1991): G created earrings made of freeze-dried foetuses for an art exhibition. The point was to comment on abortion but the defendants were guilty of outraging public decency as there was no need to prove that their act was intentional or reckless.

The role of mens rea

- Initial presumption in favour of *mens rea* is a basic element of criminal liability.

The Gammon test

Although a Privy Council decision and therefore of only persuasive authority, this case has been accepted as containing important principles. The presumption in favour of *mens rea* can be displaced if:

- this is the clear or necessary implication from the statutory words
- the offence is not 'truly criminal'
- the offence is of social concern
- the offence will help to enforce the law through greater vigilance.

Wording of the Act

- Judges look at the statute for guidance. Words such as 'knowingly' or 'intentionally' mean the section does not create a strict liability offence.
- A section is read in the context of the whole statute – if *mens rea* is mentioned in other sections but not the one at issue, an implication for strict liability may be drawn.

Quasi-criminal offences

- Many offences are regulatory to encourage good behaviour.
- Not the same as true crimes; examples include the preparation and selling of food, building regulations, licensing regulations and pollution.

Strict liability penalties

- Fines are most common.
- If imprisonment is a possibility an offence is less likely to be one of strict liability.
- Exceptions to this rule are seen as unjust.

An area of social concern

- Used to drive up standards.
- Ranges from the possession of firearms to the transmission of unlicensed broadcasts.

Conflict with human rights

- Conviction can be very easy.
- Lack of fault and acceptable defences can infringe basic human rights.

Easy enforcement of the law

- Can promote better behaviour and higher vigilance.
- Provides a deterrent.

Changing trends

- There has been a move away from strict liability in areas such as sexual offences.

Key cases on strict liability

Case	Summary facts	Area of strict liability at issue	Point of law in case
Sweet v Parsley (1969)	D rented farmhouse to tenants who smoked cannabis. D charged with being concerned in management of premises used for smoking cannabis resin	Presumption for *mens rea* Changing trend	If statutory section silent on *mens rea*, need for it is presumed
Gammon (Hong Kong) Ltd v AG of Hong Kong (1984)	Deviating from building plans was breach of Hong Kong planning laws	Creation of a new test Penalty of imprisonment	Presumption for *mens rea* can be displaced in certain situations
Pharmaceutical Society of GB v Storkwain (1986)	S charged under s58(2) Medicines Act 1968 with supplying drugs without doctor's prescription as it was forged	Statutory wording	Read statute as whole and, unlike other sections, relevant section silent as to *mens rea*, therefore strict liability imposed
Sherras v De Rutzen (1895)	Defendant's daughter sold alcohol to constable on duty – no way of knowing due to lack of police armband	Statutory wording	Not automatic that section without reference to *mens rea* creates strict liability offence
Muhamad (2002)	M charged with materially contributing to the extent of insolvency by gambling	Statutory wording Penalty of imprisonment	Section under which M charged said nothing about *mens rea* and strict liability presumed
Wings Ltd v Ellis (1984)	Room provided by holiday company did not match brochure description	Quasi-criminal offence	Strict liability offence as designed to raise standards and protect consumers
Alphacell v Woodward (1972)	Company charged with letting polluted water run into river	Quasi-criminal offence	Offence even though company did not know of pollution and had not been negligent
B v DPP (2000)	B convicted of inciting child under 14 to commit act of gross indecency	Penalty of imprisonment Changing trend	Likelihood of strict liability decreased as crime more serious in sentence and stigma
Howells (1977)	H charged with possessing firearm without certificate	Penalty of imprisonment Area of social concern	Risk to public outweighed severity of possible sentence
Blake (1997)	B was DJ convicted of broadcasting without licence	Area of social concern	Need to regulate behaviour and ensure that emergency services not interrupted
K (2001)	K had consensual sex with girl he believed 16 or over but was in fact 14	Human rights Changing trend	On question of defence of mistake, offence was not incompatible with Article 6 right to a fair trial
G (2008)	G was 15 and had sex with girl aged 12 but he reasonably believed her older as she told him she was 15. G was charged with rape of child under 13	Human rights	Offence strict liability and no breach of human rights despite consent of the girl and G's reasonable belief in her consent and age
Lim Chin Aik v The Queen (1963)	L convicted of remaining in Singapore when prohibited from entering	Easy enforcement	L had no knowledge of prohibition and not strict liability as offence did not make law more effective
Kumar (2004)	K had consensual sex with boy aged 14 after meeting him at club where policy to admit only over-18s	Changing trend	K conviction quashed on basis that honest mistake should be defence

Reform proposals for strict liability

- Make every offence clear in its *mens rea* requirements.
- Include a defence of all due diligence in every offence, as is the case in Australia and Canada.
- Move to administrative law.

Points for an essay on strict liability

- Enforcement of standards:
  - Positive – easy way to improve behaviour.
  - Negative – someone can be convicted without knowledge.
- Encourages good behaviour:
  - Positive – makes people try harder.
  - Negative – big businesses may think improvement is financially viable and individuals are often disproportionately affected.
- Speed of judicial process:
  - Positive – cases are dealt with quickly and conviction is likely.
  - Negative – can be too easy to convict.
- Use of regulatory bodies:
  - Positive – generates jobs and encourages compliance.
  - Negative – overall cost is high and bodies have considerable discretion.
- Expense:
  - Positive – most cases heard by magistrates.
  - Negative – expense loaded instead towards regulatory systems.
- Sentences:
  - Positive – penalties are usually only financial.
  - Negative – some offences can result in prison sentence; financial penalties are often punitive for small businesses and individuals.
- Stigma:
  - Positive – characterises behaviour that will not be tolerated.
  - Negative – too little effect on big companies who apologise easily, but disproportionately detrimental for individuals and small businesses.
- Defences:
  - Positive – now some use of due diligence or acceptance of mistake.
  - Negative – such defences are few and far between.
- Human rights:
  - Positive – everyone is protected by higher standards.
  - Negative – lack of *mens rea* and some punitive penalties counter basic human rights.
- Culpability and moral issues:
  - Positive – ensures necessary conviction and usually little moral content.
  - Negative – goes against basic principles of fault and blameworthiness, leading to new emphasis in areas such as sexual offences.
- Construction of offences:
  - Positive – Parliament using social paternalism.
  - Negative – many created by delegated legislation so lack of knowledge and clarity.
- Need for reform:
  - Positive – helpful to tighten up wording, introduce defences and move out of criminal law.
  - Negative – very little happened except small growth in defences.

Check your understanding

1. Approximately how many strict liability offences are there in the English legal system?
2. Give a simple definition, and an example, of strict liability.
3. Give a simple definition, and an example, of absolute liability.
4. Why is the case of *Gammon* so important in strict liability?
5. What is meant by a regulatory offence? Is this a workable definition?

Now test yourself

Tested ☐

1. Look at the following chart and decide if a strict liability offence has been committed by putting a tick in the correct column.

Act	Strict liability offence occurs	Strict liability offence does not occur
Sue gives a rabbit to Mark. Mark cooks the rabbit and eats it. Mark is very ill.		
Sue is an architect who designs an eco-friendly house for a client, Dan. Dan builds the house but takes some shortcuts to save money. Dan sells the house to Freda. Freda has lived in the house for a week when the roof falls in.		
Stefan is a barman. Jude wants to buy a drink and Stefan asks to see proof of his age. Jude shows Stefan an ID card which says he is 19. In fact Jude is 15 but looks older. Stefan sells Jude a pint of lager.		
Kevin has a business which takes water from the local river and pumps it back into the river when the steel his factory is making has been processed. Fred is employed to keep the filters clean but goes on holiday for two weeks without telling Kevin. The filters are not cleaned and toxins leak into the river, killing fish and some swans.		
Kevin sacks Fred and instead employs Guy to clean the filters. One night vandals break in and tip into the river some of the chemicals used to process the steel, killing fish and some swans.		
Kevin's factory is on a big industrial estate near an airport. A terrorist plants a bomb on the estate, intending to blow up the airport. The blast explodes some of the chemical containers Kevin is storing and chemicals go into the river, killing fish and several swans.		
Buy-Wise supermarket is supplied with pork pies by HappyPies. Harry buys a pie and suffers food poisoning.		

2. Copy the table below and then fill in the details to test your knowledge. Make a revision chart with the cases grouped appropriately.

Case name	Factual key words	Area of strict liability	Legal importance
Winzar v CC of Kent (1983)			
Alphacell v Woodward (1972)			
Sweet v Parsley (1969)			
Blake (1997)			
Gammon v AG of Hong Kong (1984)			
Kumar (2004)			
Cundy v Le Cocq (1884)			
B v DPP (2000)			
PS of GB v Storkwain (1986)			

(Continued)

(Continued)

Case name	Factual key words	Area of strict liability	Legal importance
Prince (1875)			
Lim Chin Aik v The Queen (1963)			
Larsonneur (1933)			
Wings Ltd v Ellis (1984)			
G (2008)			
Harrow LBC v Shah & Shah (1999)			
K (2001)			
Howells (1977)			
Callow v Tillstone (1900)			
Sherras v De Rutzen (1895)			
Muhamad (2002)			
Hibbert (1869)			

Exam summary

✔ **Section A** – strict liability stands alone and contains lots of AO2. A good structure is vital so be guided by the question. Even when all areas of the topic are covered, a pre-prepared answer may be less impressive than one which fully answers the question. Cases are important so use them accurately and support them with relevant AO2. There is a lot to write so pay close attention to time limits.

✔ **Section B** and **Section C** – practise applying principles in a logical and deductive way.

Striving for an A/A*?

1. **Section A** – be flexible in your essay writing: a revision mind map covering the key points will serve as a plan you can adapt to get the focus right. Remember to develop points – looking at counter-arguments is useful here.

2. Take your research further, for example, you can read an interesting article which suggested a greater role for strict liability in the criminal law at **http://www.fevr.org/new/wp-content/uploads/2010/12/Strict-liability-discussion-paper-April-2008.pdf**. You can also read interesting views on the debate between strict liability offences and human rights legislation at **http://ukhumanrightsblog.com/2011/09/28/strict-liability-for-offence-of-under-age-sex-does-not-offend-presumption-of-innocence**. You can read about potential defences by looking at the Tobacco Advertising and Promotion Act 2002 at **http://www.legislation.gov.uk/ukpga/2002/36/section/5**.

3. **Section C** – respond to each individual statement, reaching a conclusion, and remember that it is enough to apply principles rather than details of cases you have learned.

4 Attempt

This chapter relates to three key areas:

- *actus reus*
- *mens rea*
- impossibility.

What is an attempt in law? Revised ☐

- Someone tries to commit a crime but fails.

Example

White (1910): W, intending to kill his mother, put cyanide in her drink but she died of a heart attack before she touched the drink. W was not guilty of murder as he had not killed his mother but he was guilty of attempted murder.

Why is there a law on attempt? Revised ☐

- If the law could not act until the victim was injured or killed this would be unjust.
- It helps society feel safe.
- It helps the police do their job.

The old law on attempt Revised ☐

There were several common law tests, as described below.

Last act or proximity

- Defendant liable if he had done the very last act before the crime proper.
- Liability occurred very late, creating dangerous situations.
- Difficult to decide when enough had been done.

Example

Robinson (1915): a jeweller insured his stock, hid it and then made it look as if his shop had been burgled. His conviction for attempting to obtain money by false pretences was quashed as he had not got an insurance claim form, filled it in or sent it off.

Rubicon test

- Defendant crossed the line into criminality and passed the point of no return with no chance of going back.
- Difficult to prove and could be very late in a set of events.

Examples

Stonehouse (1978): S took out life insurance policies, hoping his wife would claim on them, and then faked his own death to go and live with his mistress in Australia. He was convicted of attempting to obtain insurance money by false pretences even though his wife made no claim.

Widdowson (1986): W attempted to obtain services by deception when he applied for hire purchase to buy a van using a false identity. His conviction was quashed as he was too far away from the full offence and had not crossed the Rubicon.

Series of acts test

● Defendant did several things which together created liability.

● Difficult to decide what and how many acts are enough for liability.

The current law on attempt

Revised ☐

● To clarify the situation Parliament passed the Criminal Attempts Act 1981:

   ● s1(1) – if, with an intent to commit an offence to which this section applies, a person does an act which is more than merely preparatory to the commission of the offence, he is guilty of attempting to commit the offence.

> **Typical mistake**
>
> It is counter-productive to spend too long on the old law. Although an awareness of the old law's problems gives valuable context for **Section A**, there is no need to refer to the old law in **Section B** or **Section C**.

> **Exam tip**
>
> Learn definitions and their statutory source to make your answer confident and authoritative.
>
> **Section A** – outline knowledge of the old law and its problems to show why Parliament had to act, but focus on the law and issues post 1981. Use key cases confidently and explain the law clearly, balancing this with AO2 analysis.

Actus reus of attempt – key elements

● An act which is more than merely preparatory to the commission of the full offence.

● A positive act.

Key cases in which the act is merely preparatory

Case name	Summary facts	Offence being attempted	Legal point
Gullefer (1987)	G placed bet at dog race then tried to stop race to get money back when clear dog would lose	Theft	G not embarked on crime proper
Campbell (1990)	C seen loitering outside post office. When stopped by police C had sunglasses, imitation gun and threatening note	Robbery	C still preparing
Geddes (1996)	G found hiding in school toilets with bag containing knife, rope and tape	False imprisonment	G not actually tried to commit offence

Key cases in which the act is more than merely preparatory

Case name	Summary facts	Offence being attempted	Legal point
Boyle and Boyle (1987)	B and B found standing by door with broken lock and hinge	Burglary	B and B had carried out sufficient series of acts to be attempt
Jones (1990)	J got into car wearing crash helmet and pointed shotgun at man	Murder	Getting into car and pointing gun enough for attempt

(Continued)

(Continued)

Case name	Summary facts	Offence being attempted	Legal point
AG's Reference (No 1 of 1992) (1993)	Man dragged girl into shed and attempted rape but could not get erection	Rape	Man not performed last act but had done enough
Tosti and White (1997)	T and W caught examining barn padlock with cutting equipment hidden in hedge	Burglary	By examining padlock men trying to commit full offence

Mens rea of attempt

- Normally intention is the key level of *mens rea* in an attempt.
- Recklessness is generally insufficient – but there is an exception!

Key cases on mens rea of attempt

Case name	Summary facts	Offence being attempted	Legal point
Whybrow (1951)	W wired up soap dish in bath intending to electrocute wife	Murder	Court of Appeal held that there needed to be an intention to kill for attempted murder
Easom (1971)	E picked up, looked in and replaced handbag in cinema without taking anything	Theft	E not convicted as no intention to steal particular items
Husseyn (1977)	H loitered near van containing sub-aqua equipment but ran off when saw police	Theft	H not convicted as no intention to steal particular items
Millard and Vernon (1987)	M and V kept pushing at fence in football stand	Criminal damage	No conviction as M and V only reckless
AG Ref (No 3 of 1992) (1994)	Man threw petrol bomb at car containing four men but missed	Committing arson with intent to endanger life	Needed intention to damage property but recklessness as to whether life endangered was sufficient

Attempt and impossibility

- Before the Criminal Attempts Act 1981:
    - If the crime was physically or legally impossible to commit there was no offence.
- After the Criminal Attempts Act 1981:
    - Factual impossibility: s1(2) – a person may be guilty of attempting to commit an offence even though the facts are such that the commission of the offence is impossible.
    - Legal impossibility: s1(3) – in any cases where (a) apart from this subsection a person's intention would not be regarded as having amounted to an intent to commit an offence; but (b) if the facts of the case had been as he believed them to be, his intention would be so regarded then for the purposes of subsection (1) he shall be regarded as having an intent to commit that offence.

Key cases on impossibility

Case name	Summary facts	Offence being attempted	Legal point
Anderton v Ryan (1985)	R bought video recorder thinking it was stolen but it was not	Handling stolen goods	Video player not stolen so R's act 'innocent'
Shivpuri (1986)	S intended to receive suitcase which was believed to contain drugs but actually contained harmless vegetable matter	Knowingly concerned in dealing in prohibited drugs	S intended to deal in drugs and impossibility no barrier to conviction, overruling Anderton v Ryan
Jones (2007)	J tried to solicit young girls for sex and met Amy who he thought was aged 12 but she was an under-cover policewoman	Inciting child under 13 to engage in sexual activity	J argued Amy was not real so offence impossible but was convicted

Check your understanding

1. What section of the Criminal Attempts Act 1981 defines an attempt?
2. What phrase is used in the Act in relation to the *actus reus*?
3. What level of *mens rea* is normally required for an attempt?
4. Which sections of the Criminal Attempts Act 1981 deal with impossibility and what are the two different types?
5. When did the Law Commission propose changes to the law?

Now test yourself

Tested

1. Look at the chart and, using both the old and the current law, decide when the *actus reus* of an attempt occurs. Use a different colour for each test.

Act	Actus reus of an attempt occurs
Sue decides to kill Paul	
Sue persuades her friend Richard to lend her his gun	
Sue goes into the local woods to practise using the gun	
Sue watches Paul for several days to see what time he leaves for work	
Sue goes to Paul's house with the gun and hides in the bushes before it is time for him to leave for work	
Sue loads the gun and waits	
When Paul comes out of the house Sue takes the safety catch off the gun and puts her finger on the trigger	
As Paul starts his car Sue fires the gun but misses Paul	

This exercise shows three things:

- the complexity of the old tests
- how difficult it was to create the new law in 1981
- the significance of the jury's role.

2. It is important to use cases in your answers, so copy the table below and for each of the cases shown, insert key words that show you have matched the correct case to its name. Then summarise why each case is important.

Case name	Factual key words	Area of law	Legal importance
Easom (1971)			
Jones (2007)			
Campbell (1990)			
Anderton v Ryan (1985)			
AG Ref (No 3 of 1992) (1994)			
AG's Reference (No 1 of 1992) (1993)			
Gullefer (1987)			
Tosti and White (1997)			
Geddes (1996)			
Boyle and Boyle (1987)			
Husseyn (1977)			
Shivpuri (1986)			
Millard and Vernon (1987)			
Jones (1990)			

3. For each of the following scenarios decide whether an attempted offence has taken place and give a brief justification for your answer.

   i) Brian wants to kill his wife, Carole. He puts some rat poison in Carole's coffee. Later Carole tells Brian she has a stomach ache.

   ii) Sally sees a rucksack in the gym changing room. She is short of cash and looks in the rucksack, hoping to find money. All that is in the rucksack is a pair of trainers so Sally puts the rucksack back where she found it.

   iii) Rupert is travelling back from Thailand and he intends to import some heroin which he is going to sell to cover his debts. He is stopped at customs and a packet of white powder in his luggage is tested. The powder is flour mixed with crushed aspirin.

   iv) William is caught by police in a churchyard. He has a ladder with him and a crowbar in his hand which he has used to break a padlock on the church gate.

Points for an essay on attempt

- Clarity since the CAA:
    - Positive – now only one test.
    - Negative – juries can still be unsure, leading to inconsistency.
- Justification based on high level of *mens rea*:
    - Positive – gives credibility to law.
    - Negative – harsh sentencing when harm has not occurred.
- Tough sentencing:
    - Positive – encourages public confidence.
    - Negative – arguably harsh for minimal action.
- Effective deterrent:
    - Positive – severity of crime makes a potential offender think twice.
    - Negative – little evidence that offenders consider consequences.
- Attempted murder:
    - Positive – those who fail to kill still receive most serious sentence.
    - Negative – harder to convict for attempted murder than for full offence.
- Level of *mens rea* can be higher than for full offence:
    - Positive – gives justification for punishment.
    - Negative – can be hard to convict and appears illogical.
- Effectiveness of public protection:
    - Positive – people feel safer as police can act before harm occurs.
    - Negative – difficult to know when to intervene; policy factors are highly influential.
- Need for change:
    - Positive – use US test 'alternative steps … strongly corroborative of actor's purpose'.
    - Negative – possibly changing one set of problems for another.
- Potential reform – 2007 Law Commission Consultation Paper:
    - Positive – creates new offences of reaching last act needed to commit offence and criminal preparation: same maximum penalty as full offence, could be committed by omission and need intent/conditional intent.
    - Negative – 2009 Law Commission report drops new offences but says amendment to existing law worth pursuing.

Exam summary

✔ **Section A** – attempt is reasonably compact and there is plenty of AO2. Be sure to cover all aspects as even a question which mentions a specific element, such as *actus reus*, is likely to require consideration of the other elements too. Link AO1 and AO2 to make your answer more informed, confident and coherent and try to look at an issue from more than one perspective.

✔ **Section B** – attempt is likely to be one element among several to be considered. Accurate explanation and application of current law is needed and be thorough and methodical so as not to miss an important point.

✔ **Section C** – consider whether there is an *actus reus* before moving on to *mens rea* and impossibility or a relevant defence before reaching a conclusion.

✔ Do not dwell too long on the law before 1981 or on the facts of cases as this will reduce the time available to cover what is important to score high marks.

Striving for an A/A*?

1. Take your research further, for example, read the Law Commission report starting at p.121: **http://www.justice. gov.uk/lawcommission/docs/lc318_Conspiracy_and_Attempts_Report.pdf**.

2. **Section A** – work at developing analytical points and responding to the question.

3. **Section B** – be thorough, confident and clear in your application of relevant law. Do not imagine facts and be as decisive as possible.

4. **Section C** – be disciplined, logical and precise for each individual statement.

5 Murder and defences

This chapter relates to three key areas:

- murder
- loss of control
- diminished responsibility.

What is murder in law?

Revised

- A common law offence.
- The unlawful killing of a reasonable person in being under the King's/ Queen's Peace, with malice aforethought, express or implied.
- Applies to a murder committed by a British citizen in any country.

Why is there a law on murder with defences?

Revised

- The taking of life strikes at the heart of a legal system.
- Such a law is a sign of a civilised society.
- Important to do justice and to protect, but also to deal with offenders fairly.

Actus reus of murder

Revised

Unlawful killing

- An act or an omission – see Chapter 1, p. 10.
- A killing may give rise to a defence of self-defence – see Chapter 10, p. 78.
- A killing may give rise to a defence of necessity – see Chapter 9, p. 71.

Causation

- Murder is a result crime so there must be a chain of causation – see Chapter 1, p. 13.

A human being

- When life starts is problematic.

Example

Attorney General's Reference (No 3 of 1994) (1997): a man stabbed his pregnant girlfriend. She recovered but her baby was born prematurely at seven months and died four months later. Man charged with murder and acquitted as the trial judge held that there was no liability for murder or manslaughter. The HL said in *obiter dicta* that violence to a foetus which led to harm once born alive could create criminal responsibility.

- Being brain dead is the usual recognised test for death, with no time limit on the occurrence of death, although the Attorney General has to give permission for a prosecution if it is more than three years after the original attack.

King's/Queen's peace

- Killing of an enemy in time of war is not murder.

Mens rea of murder

Revised

Malice aforethought

- Express – an intention to kill.
- Implied – an intention to cause GBH.
- Direct intent – the defendant wants to cause death or GBH and death results – see Chapter 2, p. 17.
- Oblique intent – the defendant's main aim is not to cause death or GBH but this occurs – see Chapter 2, p. 17.
- Transferred malice – see Chapter 2, p. 22.

Problems in the law of murder

Revised

Law Commission – Murder, Manslaughter and Infanticide (Report Law Com 304) 2006

The Law Commission stated the law 'is a rickety structure set upon shaky foundations' and identified some areas of particular concern:

- Development has been piecemeal and, other than s8 Criminal Justice Act 1967, Parliament has had no involvement.
- An intention to cause GBH resulting in death makes murder very broad and potentially unfair as the defendant may not realise that death could occur.
- Reasonable force can provide a complete defence but if the force is decided to be excessive there is no defence at all. Consequently some defendants appear less blameworthy if they have an honest, but unreasonable, belief as to the amount of force they need to use, but are treated the same as the most calculating of murderers.
- Duress is no defence even though a person might find themselves in an extreme situation where they are forced to act.
- The mandatory life sentence makes reflecting blameworthiness very difficult; although the judge can give minimum sentences this does not separate categories of defendants.
- There is a lot of pressure on the jury which can affect their decision-making.

They proposed two offences:

- First degree murder – the defendant intends to kill or to cause serious harm and is aware their conduct poses a serious risk of death – mandatory life sentence.
- Second degree murder – the defendant intends to do serious injury but is not aware there is a serious risk of death – maximum penalty of life.

The Government 2008 Consultation Paper Murder, Manslaughter and Infanticide: proposals for reform of the law, CP 19/08 rejected the idea of a two-tier offence but a change for those who use excessive force in self-defence came in the Coroners and Justice Act 2009.

Euthanasia

Under the present law 'mercy killing' or 'assisted dying' is unlawful, the only exception being the situation where doctors can withdraw treatment.

> **Exam tip**
>
> **Section A** – read the question carefully in order to focus on the correct aspect of the offence. Remember that comment and analysis is essential to support your knowledge.
>
> **Section B** – the elements of the offence and their application are vital. Factual material can be confined to that which is up to date. Highlight key terms to make sure you do what the question has asked for.

Loss of control

Revised

- Partial defence.
- Only for murder.
- Avoids the mandatory life sentence if successful.

    s54 – 'where the defendant (D) kills or is a party to the killing of another (V) D is not to be convicted of murder if:

a) D's acts and omissions in doing or being a party to the killing resulted from D's loss of self-control;

b) the loss of self-control had a qualifying trigger; and

c) a person of D's age and sex with a normal degree of tolerance and self-restraint and in the circumstances of D might have reacted in the same or in a similar way to D.'

Loss of self-control – s52(2) and (4)

- Must be no self-control at the time of the act which causes death.
- Loss of self-control need not be sudden.

Qualifying trigger

s55 permissible qualifying triggers are when the loss of self-control is attributable to:

- s55(3) D's fear of serious violence from V against D or another identified person; or
- s55(4) a thing or things done or said (or both) which:
    - constitute circumstances of an extremely grave character, and
    - cause D to have a justifiable sense of being seriously wronged.

Fear of violence

- Fear of violence does not need to be from the victim.
- Must be an identifiable source – a general fear is insufficient.

Things said or done

- Tighter test than under the old law of provocation.

Things excluded by the new defence

- s55(6)(c) Sexual infidelity.
- s55(6)(a) and (b) if defendant incited thing done or said out of considered desire for revenge.

Standard of self-control – s54(1)(c) and (3)

- Largely an enactment of the old provocation tests.
- Defendant's age and sex are relevant.
- Need for a normal degree of tolerance and self-restraint.
- Objective element because circumstances whose only relevance to D's conduct is that they bear on the general capacity for tolerance or self-restraint are excluded.

Circumstances of the defendant

- A range of factors can be taken into account.
- Current examples include unemployment, depression and a history of sexual abuse.

Example

R v Clinton, Parker, Evans (2012) – *Clinton*: one of three CA appeals against murder convictions by husbands arguing that loss of control should take account of sexual infidelity. C was obsessive and suspicious. C's wife left him and he found evidence of her sexual infidelity on Facebook. When she returned home to sort out bills C killed her. C took naked photos of her, texted them to her new partner and was found by police in the loft with a rope round his neck saying he was hearing voices. The trial judge did not allow loss of control to go to the jury as sexual infidelity is excluded by the 2009 Act and there was no other evidence capable of being a qualifying trigger. C was convicted of murder after the jury rejected diminished responsibility. In the CA Lord Justice Judge made several important points about loss of control:

1. The old law is irrelevant.
2. Sexual infidelity is to be disregarded as a qualifying trigger (a thing done). However, the context of the infidelity is not excluded if its effects are sufficiently serious on an objective basis to be a qualifying trigger.
3. Verbal admissions of sexual infidelity or evidence of such are also excluded (a thing said).
4. Under the objective test in s54(1)(c) the impact of sexual infidelity is not excluded when looking at the circumstances in which the defendant has reacted and lost control as everything except those bearing on the general capacity for tolerance and self-restraint should be considered.

The consequence of this decision seems to be that although sexual infidelity is excluded as a qualifying trigger it is still relevant to the circumstances in which the defendant has lost control.

Example

Zebedee (2012): Z accused and claimed to have lost self-control and killed his elderly father who had Alzheimer's and was doubly incontinent, repeatedly soiling himself in the middle of the night. Z's appeal against a murder conviction failed as although there were things done they were not extremely grave.

Might have reacted in the same or similar way to the defendant

- If a jury decide that a normal person might have lost control but would not have behaved in the same way the defence will fail.

> **Exam tip**
>
> This is a complex area of law and much depends on future decisions as the old cases on provocation have been abolished.
>
> **Section A** – will probably require a comparison with the old law and the effectiveness of the reforms; to this extent only is it worth knowing some of the older cases. The new definitions are tricky and you can reproduce them verbatim but it is perfectly acceptable to give the key elements of the defence, as the essence of the defence is most important.
>
> **Section B** and **Section C** – focus on explaining and applying relevant law as it stands – there is no need for historical revisiting of old cases.

Points for an essay on loss of control

- Problems with provocation:
  - A muddle – originated in common law and developed in Homicide Act 1957.
  - Reasonable man test created injustices and its development did not reflect Parliament's intentions.
  - Very male centred.
  - Need for conduct in the heat of the moment was not necessarily a human response.
- Cases from the old law which may be relevant in an essay include:
  - *Ahluwalia (1992)* – showed old law to be strict and sexist but also acknowledged 'slow burn'. Probably no defence under 2009 Act as need for a loss of control retained.
  - *Camplin (1978)* – showed origins of reasonable man test as partly subjective. Almost certainly defence under 2009 Act using anger as a qualifying trigger.
  - *Doughty (1986)* – shows how the law has changed as D does not fulfill either qualifying trigger.
  - *Humphreys (1995)* – shows that both qualifying triggers might be applicable and is an example of cumulative provocation by things said or done.
  - *Ibrams and Gregory (1981)* – shows that killing motivated by revenge is excluded by the 2009 Act.
  - *Pearson (1992)* – shows when fear could apply as a qualifying trigger and that the fear could be of violence against another person.
  - *Smith (2000)* and *Holley (2005)* – shows the difficulties the courts got into which have hopefully been resolved by the new Act.
- Changes achieved by the new defence:
  - Wider – no need for a sudden loss of control.
  - Includes a fear of serious violence – this covers situations in which people otherwise had no defence but it may be hard to prove.
  - Narrower – sexual infidelity is excluded although this was one of the reasons for creating provocation originally.
  - Tighter – things said or done must be of an extremely grave character.
  - Restrictive – need for things said and/or done to cause a justifiable sense of being seriously wronged.
  - Compromise – Law Commission had suggested removing any need for loss of self-control to deal with a particular situation when women kill abusive partners.

Diminished responsibility

- Created by s2(1) Homicide Act 1957.
- Amended by s52 Coroners and Justice Act 2009.
- A person who kills or is a party to the killing of another is not to be convicted of murder if he was suffering from an abnormality of mental functioning which:
  - arose from a recognised medical condition
  - substantially impaired D's ability to understand the nature of his conduct or form a rational judgement or exercise self-control, and
  - provided an explanation for D's acts and omissions in doing or being a party to the killing.
- The burden of proof is on the defendant but only to the standard of a balance of probabilities.

Abnormality of mental functioning

- As under the old law, defined as 'a state of mind so different from that of ordinary human beings that the reasonable man would term it abnormal'.

Cause of abnormality of mental functioning

- 'Recognised medical condition' covers physical conditions.
- Also covers psychological conditions.
- There must be supporting medical evidence.

Substantially impaired

- A question of degree to be decided by the jury.
- Must relate to the defendant's ability to understand the nature of their conduct: it could cover automatic states, delusions and a state induced by a low mental age where there is no awareness of a situation due to severe learning difficulties.
- Must be no ability to form a rational judgement – this could include paranoia, schizophrenia and battered wife syndrome.
- Must be no ability to exercise self-control – this could cover sexual psychopaths.

Provides an explanation for conduct

- Must now be a causal link between the abnormality of mental functioning and the killing.
- Abnormality must be a significant factor.
- Need not be the only factor.

Overlap with intoxication

- Simply being intoxicated will not give rise to defence.
- Must be an abnormality of mind arising from a recognised medical condition.
- Must impair ability to understand the nature of conduct or form a rational judgement and/or exercise self-control.
- Must be a causal link to the killing.

> **Exam tip**
>
> Another complex area where much will depend on future decisions.
>
> **Section A** – will probably require comparison with the old law and evaluation of the reforms. Consider wider links with insanity, automatism and intoxication.
>
> The definition is challenging to learn but accuracy in naming and explaining the key elements is a good basis for making analytical comment in **Section A** or applying the law to hypothetical problem situations in **Section B** and **Section C**.

- The recognised medical condition of ADS (Alcohol Dependency Syndrome) can be sufficient – the jury must consider the effect of alcohol consumed as a result of the dependency, based on whether the craving for alcohol was irresistible or could be controlled.

Key cases on diminished responsibility

Case name	Factual key words	Area of defence	Legal importance
Byrne (1960)	B was a sexual psychopath who strangled and mutilated young woman	Abnormality of mental functioning	CA substituted verdict of manslaughter as medical evidence said B could not control perverted desires
Dietschmann (2003)	D killed man who was disrespectful to memory of his aunt who had recently died. D suffering from grief-induced adjustment disorder but also drunk	Substantial impairment and intoxication	HL held needed to prove was substantial impairment induced by abnormality of mind without effect of intoxication
Tandy (1989)	T was alcoholic who normally drank Cinzano or barley wine but after drinking most of a bottle of vodka killed daughter who said she had been abused by T's husband	Substantial impairment and intoxication	T appeal against murder conviction quashed as no evidence T had been injured or that drinking was involuntary
Wood (2008)	W went to flat after drinking heavily and fell asleep. W said woke to find man trying to perform oral sex on him so W killed him with meat cleaver. W was suffering from ADS but unclear whether had damaged his brain	Substantial impairment and intoxication	CA overturned W's conviction after trial judge said brain damage induced by long-term alcohol use was needed and not all W's drinking needed to be involuntary
Dowds (2012)	D and girlfriend heavy binge drinkers with violent relationship. They drank two litres of vodka and D stabbed her 60 times. D argued voluntary acute intoxication, a recognised medical condition, but D not alcoholic/alcohol dependent	Substantial impairment and intoxication	CA dismissed D's appeal as voluntary intoxication would still not give rise to a recognised medical condition

Points for an essay on diminished responsibility

- New defence takes account of modern medical knowledge and 'recognised medical condition' allows for flexibility and development.
- Improved clarity as to the aspects of mental functioning to be taken into account.
- Burden of proof still lies on the defendant which places anyone wanting to raise it at a disadvantage and could be a breach of Article 6 ECHR – someone charged with a criminal offence is innocent until proved guilty.
- Law Commission proposed the inclusion of developmental immaturity; the government rejected this as conditions such as autism and learning difficulties could fall under the umbrella of 'recognised medical conditions'.
- Difficult overlaps remain with defences such as insanity and intoxication.
- Jury reaction can still be influential – as for the Yorkshire Ripper.
- Issues as to medical evidence and believability of expert witnesses remain.

Check your understanding

1. What section of the Coroners and Justice Act 2009 defines a qualifying trigger?
2. How is a qualifying trigger defined?
3. Give the three key elements of the defence of diminished responsibility under the Coroners and Justice Act 2009.
4. What has happened to the old defence of provocation and why is this significant?
5. How is intoxication dealt with in diminished responsibility?

Now test yourself

1. Copy the table below and fill in the details to test your knowledge and then make a revision chart with the cases linked to the statutory sections.

Case name	Factual key words	Area of defence	Legal importance
Tandy (1989)			
Woods (2008)			
Dietschmann (2003)			
Clinton (2012)			
Dowds (2012)			
Byrne (1960)			
Zebedee (2012)			

Exam summary

✔ **Section A** – an essay may deal with any aspect of this topic so your revision needs to include AO2 for each. For murder you need to be equally confident with *actus reus* and *mens rea* elements, as well as reform proposals. For the new defences you need to be able to compare the current law with older provisions and cases, with analysis focusing on reform.

✔ **Section B** – for each topic you must focus on identification, explanation and application, so there is no need to use anything other than the current law. With the defences be sure you can define the provisions accurately and then apply them.

✔ **Section C** – application of legal principles is vital so check that you are confident with each step, especially in relation to the defences.

Striving for an A/A*?

1. Take your research further: look out for new cases on the defences in the 2009 Act and read in more detail about decided cases at: **http://www.bbc.co.uk/news/uk-16592680**.

2. **Section A** – think about the new defences compared to the old law. Also consider the wider picture with regard to defences which affect the mind in order to make more sophisticated points.

3. **Section B** – ensure that definitions are clear and accurate so you can apply them.

4. **Section C** – apply relevant principles concisely and logically.

6 Involuntary manslaughter

This chapter relates to three key areas:

- unlawful act or constructive manslaughter
- gross negligence manslaughter
- subjective reckless manslaughter.

What is involuntary manslaughter in law?

Revised

- The *actus reus* of murder exists but the *mens rea* is missing.
- This very broad offence can be committed in different ways.

Why is there a law on involuntary manslaughter?

Revised

- Few people set out to commit murder so involuntary manslaughter covers a range of situations in which death occurs unlawfully.
- Gives judicial discretion in sentencing which helps juries who may not like the responsibility of convicting when *mens rea* is hard to prove and the mandatory life sentence follows.

Exam tip

Involuntary manslaughter can appear in any part of the paper. Learn the test for each kind of manslaughter precisely, using relevant case examples in support.

Section A – prepare a list of analytical points looking at the way the offences work, their effectiveness and ideas for reform.

Section B and **Section C** – application of the tests will take you into the higher mark bands.

Typical mistake

The most common problem is vagueness in identifying the correct types of manslaughter and defining the elements of the tests. Another is spending too long on proving causation in **Section B**: read the question carefully to get the balance right. If the question directs you to consider manslaughter no credit will be earned for dealing with murder.

Unlawful act manslaughter (UAM)

Revised

- Also known as constructive manslaughter.
- Liability is built up from several different elements.
- Defendant may not have realised death or even injury might occur.

Unlawful act

- Must be an unlawful criminal act.
- A civil wrong is insufficient.
- An omission is insufficient.

Dangerous act

- Objective test from *Church (1966)*: an act 'such as all sober and reasonable people would inevitably recognise must subject the other person to, at least, the risk of some harm resulting there from, albeit not serious harm'.

● Does not need to be against a person.

Causing death

● See 'causation' in Chapter 1, p. 13.
● Particular problem exists in relation to cases involving drugs.

Mens rea

● Must be *mens rea* for the initial unlawful act.
● Defendant need not realise their act is unlawful or dangerous.

Key cases on unlawful act manslaughter

Case name	Summary facts	Element of UAM	Legal point
Franklin (1883)	F threw box off pier into sea which hit and killed swimmer	Criminal act	F not liable for manslaughter as only a civil wrong
Lowe (1973)	L convicted of wilful neglect and manslaughter of baby son	Criminal act	L's conviction for manslaughter quashed as no act when L failed to care for child
Lamb (1967)	L killed friend with a revolver containing two bullets but both believed gun would not fire	Criminal act	L not liable as no assault since friend did not fear violence and L believed no bullet would fire
Larkin (1943)	Woman killed when fell on to cut-throat razor L brandishing at another man	Dangerous act	L's conviction for manslaughter upheld as threatening to assault man and objectively dangerous as someone likely to be injured
Mitchell (1983)	M hit man in post office queue. He fell into 89-year-old woman who died	Dangerous act Causing death	M's act objectively dangerous even though someone other than original person suffered harm
Goodfellow (1986)	G set fire to council house and killed three people	Dangerous act Causing death	G's conviction upheld although unlawful act was against property
Dawson (1985)	D and another held up petrol station with masks, sticks and fake gun. Attendant with heart condition died of heart attack	Dangerous act	D's conviction for manslaughter quashed as neither he nor reasonable man aware of victim's condition
Watson (1989)	W and another broke into home of 89-year-old man who had heart attack 90 minutes later and died	Dangerous act	W's conviction quashed on causation point but burglary dangerous act as old man's frailty obvious to reasonable man
Carey (2006)	Girl ran away from gang who attacked her and died of heart condition worsened by running away	Dangerous act	C's manslaughter conviction quashed as only been one punch; other factors contributed but not objectively dangerous
Cato (1976)	C and another prepared syringes containing heroin and injected each other. The man C injected died	Causing death	C was convicted of manslaughter based on unlawful act under s23 OAPA 1861
Dalby (1982)	D supplied drug to person who injected themselves and died	Causing death	D's conviction quashed as chain of causation broken by act of self-injection
Rogers (2003)	R held tourniquet around man's arm. Man self-injected drug and died	Causing death	R convicted of manslaughter using s23 OAPA 1861 as self-injection only occurred because of R
Kennedy (2007)	K prepared syringe containing heroin and gave it to person who self-injected and died	Causing death	K's manslaughter conviction quashed by HL based on self-injection
Newbury and Jones (1977)	N and J teenage boys who threw part of paving stone on to railway track, hitting train and killing guard	*Mens rea*	N and J's manslaughter convictions were upheld as only needed *mens rea* for act and no need to foresee resulting harm

Gross negligence manslaughter (GNM)

Defined by *Adomako (1995)*:

- Must be a duty of care.
- Duty breached by act or omission.
- Death must be caused.
- Breach must be so grossly negligent as to justify criminal conviction in jury's eyes.

Example

Adomako (1995): A, an anaesthetist, only noticed that the tube carrying oxygen to his patient had been disconnected for several minutes when his patient had a heart attack. The patient suffered brain damage and died six months later. A's failure was seen as 'abysmal' – a competent anaesthetist would have noticed within 15 seconds. A was convicted and appealed to the HL but his conviction was upheld.

Duty of care

- Defined by principles of negligence in *Donoghue v Stevenson (1932)* with a duty being owed to a neighbour – persons so closely and directly affected by an act that it would be reasonable to have them in contemplation at the time of the act or omission.

Breach of duty causing death

- Must be a breach.
- Must be proof of causation – see Chapter 1, p. 13.

Gross negligence

- Term is defined by the courts.
- Combines civil and criminal principles.
- Lord Hewart in *Bateman (1925)* stated gross negligence meant something which 'went beyond a mere matter of compensation between subjects and showed such disregard for the life and safety of others as to amount to a crime against the State and conduct deserving of punishment'.
- Lord Atkins in *Andrews v DPP (1937)* stated a very high degree of negligence was needed – a 'criminal disregard' for others' safety.
- Lord Mackay in *Adomako (1995)*: the jury had to decide whether, in all the circumstances, and having regard to the risk of death, the defendant's conduct was so bad as to be criminal.
- Must be a risk of death.

Key cases on gross negligence manslaughter

Case name	Summary facts	Element of GNM	Legal point
Singh (1999)	S was landlord of a property where a faulty gas fire caused death	Duty of care Breach	S convicted as duty to maintain and manage property
Litchfield (1998)	L owned and captained ship. L set sail knowing engines might fail and three of crew died	Duty of care Breach	L convicted as owed duty to crew

(Continued)

(Continued)

Case name	Summary facts	Element of GNM	Legal point
Wacker (2002)	W brought 60 illegal immigrants into UK in lorry on cross channel ferry. W closed air vent killing 58 immigrants	Duty of care Breach	W's manslaughter conviction upheld by CA as knew immigrants relied on him and owed them duty, even though enterprise criminal
Evans (2009)	E bought heroin and gave to half-sister, who self-injected. When girl collapsed E and mother put girl to bed, hoping she would recover but she died	Duty of care Breach	E and mother convicted of gross negligence manslaughter. Mother had duty to care for child and E created state of affairs in which she knew, or ought reasonably to have known, of risk to half-sister's life
Bateman (1925)	B was a doctor who attended a woman in childbirth. Despite medical problem B did not send woman to hospital for five days and she died	Gross negligence	B's manslaughter conviction was quashed
Misra and another (2004)	M and another doctor failed to identify and treat infection in patient after a knee operation, who then died	Gross negligence	CA upheld convictions as risk of death and argument that elements of gross negligence unclear and breach of ECHR Article 7 rejected

Reckless manslaughter

Revised

- Some doubt as to whether the offence exists.
- It is rarely used in practice.

Example

Lidar (2000): L and friends were asked to leave a pub. L got into his Range Rover and a man in the car shouted to the pub doorman. The doorman approached and reached in through the open passenger window. L drove off with the doorman half in the car. He was dragged under the wheels and died. L was convicted of manslaughter as he had seen the risk and decided to run it.

Reform of the law of manslaughter

Revised

- The Law Commission 2006 report Murder, Manslaughter and Infanticide states the following:
  - Second degree murder includes killings where the defendant was aware that their conduct posed a serious risk of death; and they had intent to cause either some injury, a fear of injury, or a risk of injury – this includes what is now reckless manslaughter.
  - Constructive manslaughter is defined as occurring where death is caused by a criminal act which is intended to cause injury, or where there is an awareness that the act involves a serious risk of causing injury.
  - What is now gross negligence manslaughter is defined as death occurring as a result of the defendant's conduct falling far below what could reasonably be expected in the circumstances, where there was a risk that the defendant's conduct would cause death and this risk would have been obvious to a reasonable person in the defendant's position and the defendant must have had the capacity to appreciate the risk.

Points for an essay on manslaughter

- Unlawful act manslaughter:
  - Encompasses a wide range of conduct so levels of blame can be variable.
  - Breadth of sentencing is also variable and may not match blameworthiness.
  - Possible inconsistency as some defendants appear to have seen risks in their conduct while for others death is an unexpected result.
  - Part of the test is objective. This is at odds with other areas where, using recklessness as *mens rea*, the test is subjective.
- Gross negligence manslaughter:
  - Circular test – gross negligence is assessed by whether the act is bad enough to be criminal; it is bad enough to be criminal if it is grossly negligent.
  - Jury interpretation can be inconsistent.
  - Basing criminal conviction on civil law principles may be inappropriate.
- Reckless manslaughter:
  - Criticised as to whether it exists and, if it does, whether it is useful.
- Reforms:
  - Some crimes presently classified as manslaughter would be up-graded to second degree murder. This would assist differentiation based on blameworthiness as reckless manslaughter would become second degree murder if a defendant was so reckless that they in fact intended to cause injury or a fear or risk of injury.
  - For gross negligence manslaughter it is still possible for a defendant to be convicted even if they were unaware their conduct might cause death as long as they were capable of appreciating the risk at the relevant time. However, reform would protect those who cannot appreciate the risk, perhaps through youth or mental disability.

Key terms

Unlawful act/constructive manslaughter:
- an unlawful and objectively dangerous act
- an intentional act
- an act which causes death
- a reasonable man would have seen a risk of harm.

Gross negligence manslaughter:
- a duty of care
- a breach of duty of care
- a risk of death
- conduct which is grossly negligent.

Check your understanding

1. Which case is authority for subjective reckless manslaughter?
2. Why is the case of *Newbury and Jones (1977)* important?
3. Explain one problem with the test for gross negligence manslaughter.
4. What is the problem associated with using the test explained in *Church (1963)* in unlawful act manslaughter?
5. Give three reasons why the law on manslaughter needs to be reformed.

1. Look at the chart and decide what type of manslaughter charge is most likely.

Act	Manslaughter type
Andreas offers to care for his ageing grandmother who is confined to bed. She is not always grateful for the things Andreas does for her and after an argument he takes her no food for three days. The next time Andreas goes into his grandmother's room she has died.	
Brenda is a teacher. She takes some children on a hike but does not check the route beforehand. The hike takes the children along steep cliffs. Instead of turning back Brenda tells the children to keep walking. A child falls off the cliff and is killed.	
Christine is a chef and she gets into an argument with Daphne, another chef, whom Christine accuses of being an alcoholic. Christine waves a knife at Daphne, who has been drinking. Daphne runs towards Christine but cannot keep her balance because she is drunk. She falls into Christine and on to the knife Christine is holding. Daphne dies.	
Edward is a police officer on duty in a city centre on a Saturday night. He sees a fight break out in which a man slashes a girl with a bottle. Edward sees the girl fall to the floor but he gets into his patrol car and drives off. The girl dies.	
Frank has been suspended from school and he is very angry with the headmaster. He decides to start a fire at the school. He throws a petrol bomb through a window and runs off. The school caretaker sees the flames and tries to fight the blaze but dies from smoke inhalation.	

This exercise shows two things:

● the need to be confident with each of the tests

● the ease with which types of manslaughter can be identified if the basic tests are known.

2. Copy the table below and for each of the following cases, insert key words that show you have matched the correct case to its name. Then summarise why the case is important.

Case name	Factual key words	Area of manslaughter	Legal importance
Evans (2009)			
Dalby (1982)			
Bateman (1925)			
Lidar (2000)			
Goodfellow (1986)			
Newbury and Jones (1977)			
Kennedy (2007)			
Franklin (1883)			
Litchfield (1998)			
Lamb (1967)			
Mitchell (1983)			
Larkin (1943)			
Carey (2006)			
Watson (1989)			
Adomako (1995)			

(Continued)

(Continued)

Rogers (2003)			
Misra and another (2004)			
Wacker (2002)			
Singh (1999)			
Lowe (1973)			

3. Make a revision mind map linking these cases with relevant manslaughter tests.

Exam summary

✔ Manslaughter may appear in any part of the paper.

✔ **Section A** – be as confident with reform proposals as with the law in its present state and its problems.

✔ **Section B** – the different tests must be explained clearly, supported by relevant citation and then applied accurately to the facts. Begin by identifying the types of manslaughter and do not to spend too long on causation – it is only one element of the test. Be systematic in your explanation and application in order to cover all issues. If multiple offences or persons are involved make a plan and deal with one issue or person at a time.

✔ **Section C** – a thorough knowledge of the tests is essential in order to apply the principles. Link to the scenario at every step and reach a conclusion to each statement given.

Striving for an A/A*?

1. Be 100 per cent confident with your definitions and explanations of the tests. Link to the most relevant cases, remembering that it is better to use a few well rather than to try to fit in every single case you have studied.

2. Take your research further by reading the Law Commission report, for example. There are two versions – the standard one can be found at: **http://lawcommission.justice.gov.uk/docs/lc304_Murder_Manslaughter_and_Infanticide_Report.pdf** and there is a more accessible version at **http://lawcommission.justice.gov.uk/docs/lc304_Murder_Manslaughter_and_Infanticide_Report_easyread.pdf**.

3. **Section A** – practise developing analytical points and, most importantly, be sure to respond to the question asked.

4. **Section B** – do not analyse the law – apply it!

5. **Section C** – be disciplined, logical and precise.

7 Non-fatal offences and defences

This chapter relates to three key areas:

- s39 Criminal Justice Act 1988
- s47, s20 and s18 OAPA 1861
- defence of consent.

Exam tip

Make sure you learn the statutory definitions for the accurate naming and explanation of each offence. This is a springboard for analysis in **Section A** and for correct application in **Section B** and **Section C**.

What are non-fatal offences against the person in law?

Revised

- A collection of offences that result in people being hurt to varying degrees but where they do not die.

Why is there a law on non-fatal offences against the person?

- To punish defendants.
- To send out a deterrent message.
- To protect victims and wider society against relatively common offences.

Assault

Revised

- Summary offence with a maximum penalty of six months' imprisonment or a fine of £5000, or both.
- Defined at common law.
- Charged under s39 CJA 1988.

Definition

- An act which causes the victim to apprehend the infliction of immediate, unlawful force with either an intention to cause another to apprehend immediate unlawful personal violence, or recklessness as to whether such apprehension is caused.
- An act:
  - cannot be committed by omission.
  - can extend to words or silence.

Apprehend immediate unlawful force

- Victim must apprehend that immediate force is going to be used against them.
- No offence if the defendant cannot actually use force.

Typical mistake

Many candidates spend a long time on *actus reus* but don't deal with *mens rea* fully, or do not mention it at all. With the exception of strict liability, all offences comprise both elements. Arguably *mens rea* is more important as it indicates blameworthiness. Read a question carefully as it is counter-productive to spend too long on unnecessary areas of this large topic.

- Fear is sufficient if 'imminent'.
- Words can prevent what would otherwise be an assault.

Unlawfulness of force

- Force used must be unlawful to give rise to an assault.

Mens rea

- intention to cause another to apprehend immediate unlawful personal violence; or
- recklessness as to whether such apprehension is caused – the defendant must realise that the acts/words could cause another to apprehend unlawful personal violence.

Battery   Revised ☐

- Summary offence with a maximum penalty of six months' imprisonment or a fine of £5000, or both.
- Defined at common law but charged under s39 CJA 1988.

Definition

- The application of unlawful force to another person intending either to apply unlawful physical force to another, or recklessness as to whether unlawful physical force is applied.

Application of unlawful force

- The slightest touch is enough.
- The touching of clothes is sufficient.
- The act may be continuing.
- The act may be indirect.
- In duty situations liability can occur by omission.
- The force must be unlawful.
- There is no need for an assault.

Mens rea

- intention to apply unlawful force to another, or
- recklessness as to whether unlawful force is applied – the defendant must realise there is a risk that his act or omission could cause unlawful force to be applied to another.

Key cases on assault and battery

Case name	Summary facts	Offence	Legal point
Constanza (1997)	C wrote 800 letters to victim and made phone calls. Last two letters seen as threats by victim	Assault	Assault occurred due to fear of violence
Ireland (1997)	Silent phone calls	Assault	Assault occurred by silence
Lamb (1967)	L killed friend with revolver containing two bullets but both believed gun would not fire	Assault	No assault as friend did not fear violence and L believed no bullet would be fired

(Continued)

(Continued)

Case name	Summary facts	Offence	Legal point
Smith v CC of Woking (1983)	S looked through woman's bedroom window late at night. She was scared, thinking S would break in	Assault	Assault even though S outside as woman believed what S would do was likely to be violent
Tuberville v Savage (1669)	S put hand on sword saying if judges not in town would act differently	Assault	Words nullified assault of having hand on sword
Light (1857)	L raised sword over wife's head and threatened her	Assault	Assault as wife feared force and words did not negate fear
Collins v Wilcock (1984)	Police asked woman to get into car for questioning but she walked off. Officer grabbed woman to detain her but she scratched officer's arm	Battery	Conviction of assaulting police officer in execution of duty quashed. Officer held arm unlawfully as no arrest and woman entitled to get free
Wood (Fraser) v DPP (2008)	Man believed to be Fraser threw ashtray in pub and police officer took hold of W who matched the description. As W tried to pull away another officer grabbed W's other arm	Battery	Conviction of assaulting two officers in execution of duty quashed. Force used to detain not arrest so W entitled to struggle
Thomas (1985)	T rubbed hem of woman's skirt	Battery	T conviction upheld as touching clothes same as touching person
Fagan (1969)	When F directed to park by policeman wheel of car went on officer's foot. Asked to move but F turned engine off for several minutes	Battery	*Actus reus* occurred when F drove car on to foot. *Mens rea* occurred when intended not to move car and offence completed when ignition turned off
Martin (1881)	M placed bar across theatre doorway, turned off lights and shouted, 'Fire!' Several people injured	Battery	M was convicted even though did not touch anyone directly
DPP v K (1990)	K was a schoolboy who stole acid and hid it in hot air hand drier used by another boy who was burned	Battery	K's conviction quashed but Divisional Court QBD said battery could be indirect
Haystead v CC of Derbyshire (2000)	H punched woman who let go of child she was holding and child injured by fall	Battery	H liable as reckless whether act would injure child
DPP v Santana-Bermudez (2003)	Policewoman asked S if had sharp objects before search. S said not but policewoman injured by needle in S's pocket	Battery	Failure of S to tell truth created liability
A v UK (1998)	A beat son with garden cane	Battery	A acquitted by jury but European Court of Human Rights said UK law offended Article 3 ECHR

Assault occasioning actual bodily harm – s47 OAPA 1861

Revised

- Triable either way offence with a maximum penalty of five years.

Definition

- An assault or battery which causes actual bodily harm, with the intention to cause the victim to fear unlawful force, or to subject unlawful force, or to be subjectively reckless as to whether the victim fears or is subjected to unlawful force.

Actual bodily harm

- *Miller (1954)* – 'any hurt or injury calculated to interfere with the health or comfort of the victim'. A short lack of consciousness is sufficient – *T v DPP (2003)*.
- Includes injuries such as bruises, scratches and grazes.
- Psychiatric harm must give rise to a recognised medical condition and be more than 'mere emotions' – *Chan Fook (1997)*.

Mens rea

- Intention or subjective recklessness as to whether the victim fears or is subjected to unlawful force.
- No need to prove any *mens rea* for the ABH.

Malicious wounding/inflicting grievous bodily harm – s20 OAPA 1861

Revised

- Triable either way offence with a maximum penalty of five years.

Definition

- 'Whosoever shall unlawfully and maliciously wound or inflict any GBH upon another person, either with or without a weapon or instrument.'

Wound or GBH

- Either is sufficient.
- GBH: *DPP v Smith (1961)* – really serious harm, but serious harm since *Saunders (1985)* and seriousness is assessed in light of the victim's age and health.
- Wound – a cut or break in the continuity of the whole skin.
- Harm can be psychiatric.
- Harm can be a disease.

Inflicting

- No need for a technical assault or battery.
- No practical difference between 'inflict' in s20 and 'cause' in s18.

Mens rea

- Maliciously – intention to do the kind of harm that was done or foresight of the kind of harm that might be done and a decision to take that risk assessed subjectively using the *Cunningham* test.
- Need to foresee harm but not necessarily the serious harm that results.

Wounding or causing grievous bodily harm with intent – s18 OAPA 1861

Revised

- Indictable offence with a maximum sentence of life.

Definition

- 'Whosoever shall unlawfully and maliciously by any means whatsoever wound or cause any GBH to any person, with intent to do some GBH to any person, or with intent to resist or prevent the lawful apprehension or detainer of any person ...'

Actus reus

- A wound.
- Grievous bodily harm.
- D's act must be a substantial cause of the wound or GBH.

Mens rea

- Intention to do some GBH or an intention to resist or prevent the lawful apprehension or detention of any person.
- No need to specifically prove malice.
- Must be specific intent to resist or prevent arrest but recklessness as to the wound or injury caused is sufficient.

Reform proposals for OAPA offences   Revised ☐

- 1998 Home Office Consultation Document, Violence: Reforming the Offences Against the Person Act 1861 – Clause 1 of the draft Bill:
  - Intentionally causing serious injury.
  - Recklessly causing serious injury.
  - Intentionally or recklessly causing injury.
  - Assault – intentionally or recklessly applying force or causing an impact to another, or causing a person to believe any such force or impact is imminent.

Key cases on OAPA offences

Case name	Summary facts	OAPA offence	Legal point
DPP v Smith (Michael) (2006)	S cut off girlfriend's ponytail during argument	s47	Divisional Court QBD held cutting substantial amount of hair sufficient
Roberts (1972)	R tried to remove coat of female hitchhiker in car. She jumped out at 30 mph and suffered cuts and bruises	s47	R convicted as intended to apply unlawful force and no *mens rea* needed for resulting ABH
Savage (1991)	S threw beer over woman in pub but glass slipped and cut woman's hand	s47	S convicted as no *mens rea* for harm but intended to apply unlawful force
Bollom (2004)	B convicted when 17-month-old child suffered bruises to abdomen, arms and leg	s20	B convicted of more serious offence based on age of victim
JCC v Eisenhower (1983)	Victim shot in eye with shotgun pellet causing severe bleeding under skin	s20	No wound as all layers of skin not broken
Wood (2008)	W broke victim's collarbone	s20	No break in skin and so no wound

(Continued)

(Continued)

Case name	Summary facts	OAPA offence	Legal point
Burstow (1997)	B carried out campaign of harassment against ex-girlfriend using abusive and silent phone calls, hate mail and stalking. Woman suffered severe depression	s20	B convicted based on level of psychiatric harm
Dica (2004)	D infected two women with HIV after unprotected sex. D did not say he was HIV positive	s20	Offence could occur by transmission of disease
Lewis (1974)	L shouted threats at wife through locked door which he tried to break down. She jumped out of second-floor window, breaking both legs	s20	L convicted as technical assault led to serious harm
Parmenter (1991)	P injured baby son by throwing him in air and said did not realise risk of injury	s20	P's 20 conviction reduced on appeal to s47 as not foreseen any injury
Morrison (1989)	Police officer grabbed M to arrest him but M leapt through window, dragging officer, who was badly cut by glass	s18	M convicted as either intended injury or realised risk of it occurring and took risk

Points for an essay on non-fatal offences

- Act is over 150 years old and language has changed.
- 'Malicious' now has a different meaning.
- Use of 'inflict' and 'cause' is unnecessarily confusing.
- Hierarchical structure makes little sense.
- Offences are not sequential.
- Assault and battery are outside the Act.
- Acceptable injuries have evolved, especially with regard to disease and psychiatric harm.
- *Mens rea* for s47 is the same as for assault or battery despite s47 leading to a higher maximum sentence.
- Small change in level of harm can have large effect on offence charged.
- Sentence is the same for s47 and s20 although both *actus reus* and *mens rea* are more serious for s20.
- Difficulty of defining wound and GBH is unsatisfactory.
- Possible to be convicted for s18 even if only minor injury foreseen as long as arrest is resisted.
- Reform proposals have not been enacted and reckless causing of serious injury by transmission of disease would not be an offence.

Check your understanding

1. Give a simple definition of assault.
2. Give a simple definition of battery.
3. What level of *mens rea* is needed for s47 OAPA 1861?
4. What is the difference between a wound and GBH?
5. What level of *mens rea* is needed for s20 OAPA 1861?

Now test yourself

1. Look at the chart and decide on the most appropriate non-fatal offence against the person in each of the situations described.

Act	Non-fatal offence
Sue has fallen out with her neighbour, Paul. Sue goes to Paul's house with a knife in her pocket. When he opens the door she stabs him in the stomach.	
Richard is drunk in a city park. A policeman tries to arrest him and Richard head butts the policeman, breaking the policeman's nose.	
Kate is washing up when she sees a stranger, Colin, in her garden. Colin is staring through the window at her.	
Dave is walking his dog when Keith comes past on his mountain bike. Keith pushes Dave, who falls over and grazes his knee.	
Albert is beaten by Fred in a local gardening competition to grow the biggest marrow. Albert waves his spade at Fred who trips and Albert's spade cuts Fred's head very badly.	

2. Copy the table below and insert key words that show you have matched the correct case to its name. Then summarise why the case is important.

Case name	Factual key words	Area of law	Legal importance
Dica (2004)			
Lamb (1967)			
Lewis (1974)			
Collins v Wilcock (1984)			
Martin (1881)			
Morrison (1989)			
DPP v Smith (2006)			
Constanza (1997)			
Parmenter (1991)			
Light (1857)			
Roberts (1972)			
Ireland (1997)			
Wood (F) v DPP (2008)			
Burstow (1997)			
Smith v CC Woking (1980)			
Eisenhower (1983)			
Turberville v Savage (1669)			
Fagan (1969)			
Savage (1991)			
Santana-Bermudez (2003)			
DPP v K (1990)			
Bollom (2004)			
Thomas (1985)			
A v UK (1998)			
Haystead (2000)			

3. Make a revision mind map linking the cases shown in the table to the relevant offences and their definitions.

Exam practice – Section C question

Sergei is driving his car at speed. Dasha, a pedestrian, has to leap out of Sergei's way and she falls over, suffering cuts and bruises. Adrian, a passerby, helps Dasha to her feet. Dasha's boyfriend, Miroslav, sees Dasha fall. He runs over and shouts at Adrian, 'Let go of her or die!' Miroslav drags Sergei from the car and kicks him repeatedly, breaking three of Sergei's ribs.

Evaluate the accuracy of *each* of the four statements A, B, C and D individually, as they apply to the facts in the above scenario.

● Statement A: Sergei will be liable for a section 20 OAPA 1861 offence.

● Statement B: Sergei will be liable for a section 47 OAPA 1861 offence.

● Statement C: Miroslav will not be guilty of an assault on Adrian.

● Statement D: Miroslav will be liable for a section 18 OAPA 1861 offence.

(Objective reasoning/dilemma board question – AO2 – 20 marks.)

Check Your answers at **www.therevisionbutton.co.uk/myrevisionnotes**

Online

Exam summary

✔ Non-fatal offences can appear in any section of the paper.

✔ **Section A** – explain both elements of each offence clearly and accurately. Use cases to illustrate your points but do not dwell on the facts. Expand AO2 points to reach the higher mark bands and link cases to show sophistication and coherence. Don't forget about reform proposals.

✔ **Section B** – identify, define, explain and apply offences clearly and precisely, covering both elements. Scenarios are often complex so make a plan and consider one offence or person at a time.

✔ **Section C** – be concise, logical and decisive. Read every statement carefully before you begin.

Defence of consent

Revised

● Negates some offences against the person.

● Occasionally leads to controversial decisions as in *Simon Slingsby* (1995) where there was no conviction when vigorous sexual activity involving a ring led to blood poisoning and death.

Elements of consent

● Must be real.

● Cannot be induced by fear.

● Can be implied for the reality of everyday life.

● Can be implied for contact sports within the rules of the game.

● Can be given for minor injuries, with limits set by public policy.

● Can be an honest mistake as to a belief in consent.

● No consent to death.

> **Exam tip**
>
> Be clear on the key elements of the defence and the principles behind it.
>
> **Section A** – your knowledge needs to be sound, together with AO2 analysis on the strengths and weaknesses of consent, its limits and reform proposals.
>
> **Section B** – practise applying the defence to a scenario of non-fatal offences.

> **Typical mistake**
>
> **Section A** – a poor balance between factual material and comment. Putting all your AO2 in one block and failing to develop points makes it hard to access the higher mark bands.
>
> **Section B** – applying irrelevant elements of the defence based on the scenario facts you are given.
>
> **Section C** – using cases and not being conclusive.

Key cases on consent

Case name	Summary facts	Element of consent	Legal point
Donovan (1934)	D caned girl for sexual gratification, causing bruising	Definition	D convictions for common assault and indecent assault quashed as consent given

(Continued)

(Continued)

Case name	Summary facts	Element of consent	Legal point
Tabassum (2000)	T measured women's breasts saying making medical database. Women consented believing T medically qualified or doing medical training	Real consent	T committed offence as women only consented to medical examination
Clarence (1888)	C had sex with wife and gave her sexually transmitted disease	Real consent	No offence as wife deemed to consent to sex with husband
Dica (2004)	D infected two women with HIV after unprotected sex. D did not tell them he was HIV positive	Real consent	D committed offence as women did not give real consent
Olugboja (1982)	Victim raped by O's companion. She had seen O rape another woman so allowed him to have sex with her and O said she consented	Real consent	CA held crucial difference between real consent and mere submission
Barnes (2004)	B made late tackle on player during amateur game leading to a serious injury	Consent in sport	B conviction quashed as not grave enough to be criminal
AG Reference (No 6 of 1980) (1981)	Street fight to settle differences	Limits of consent	No consent based on public policy
Brown (1993)	B convicted of s20 and s47 as part of adult sadomasochist group where all consented and none needed medical attention	Limits of consent	No consent based on public policy
Wilson (1996)	W branded wife's buttocks with his initials using hot knife and she needed medical treatment	Limits of consent	No offence as she asked him to do it. Branding is like tattooing and prosecution not in public interest
Jones (1986)	Two boys tossed into air by older boys. Suffered broken arm and ruptured spleen	Mistake as to consent	Could consent to rough horseplay based on honest belief
Aitken (1992)	RAF officers poured white spirit over drunk and sleeping friend wearing fire-resistant flying suit who suffered major burns	Mistake as to consent	Convictions for s20 quashed as jury should be left to decide if mistaken belief in victim's consent
Emmett (1999)	E and girlfriend had sex which resulted in haemorrhage to girlfriend's eye and burns on breast	Extent of consent	CA upheld E's conviction as harm caused more than transient or trivial
R (on the application of Pretty) v DPP (2001)	P sought declaration that her husband not be prosecuted if he assisted her suicide	Extent of consent	HL refused declaration as no consent to death

Points for an essay on consent

- Justificatory defence – avoids greater harm and promotes human autonomy but balanced by public protection needs.

- Without consent, contact sports would be illegal; can keep sports cases out of courts but injury must occur within the rules as sports players are also role models.

- In Canada sport-based defence relies on entertainment value and informed consent – *Cuerrier (1998)*.

- Essential for medical procedures, even if resulting harm is intentional and serious, in order to save life or improve quality of life. Makes emergency treatment possible if patient is unconscious.

- Public interest is difficult to balance in sexual activity cases: *Brown (1993)* is based on cruelty and degradation not being condoned, although this conflicts with Article 8 of ECHR, arguably taking social paternalism too far. In cases such as *Wilson (1996)* branding is permissible even though injury caused is serious.

- For some cases involving sexual behaviour consent is not allowed, yet some cases involving serious injury from horseplay permit consent.

- Euthanasia debate remains unresolved.

- An example of conduct not in the public interest and criminalised, even if consented to, is the Prohibition of Female Circumcision Act 1985.

Check your understanding

6. Why should consent be a defence?
7. Why was the defence not allowed in *Brown (1993)*?
8. What is the role of consent in cases involving sport?
9. Why was the defence allowed in *Wilson (1996)*?
10. Why is the decision in *Dica (2004)* important?

Now test yourself

Tested

4. Copy the table and for each of the cases below, insert key words that show you have matched the correct case to its name. Then summarise why the case is important.

Case name	Factual key words	Legal importance
Emmett (1999)		
Dica (2004)		
Donovan (1934)		
Aitken (1992)		
Barnes (2004)		
AG Ref (No 6 of 1980) (1981)		
Pretty (2001)		
Tabassum (2000)		
Jones (1986)		
Olugboja (1982)		
Wilson (1996)		
Clarence (1888)		
Brown (1993)		

5. Make a revision mind map grouping the cases into their most appropriate areas and link them to analytical points.

Exam summary

✔ **Section A** – consent is reasonably concise and there is lots of AO2. Remember to expand analytical points and be disciplined with time, even if this is your favourite topic!

✔ **Section B** – consent is likely to be part of a bigger question on non-fatal offences so be time-smart and only refer to areas relevant to the scenario facts.

✔ **Section C** – principles may be relevant as part of a wider question on non-fatal offences.

Striving for an A/A*?

1. Be really confident with the names and definitions of these complex offences, dealing with both *actus reus* and *mens rea*.

2. Take your research on non-fatal offences further. For example, read the Law Commission report and use the index on page 4 to move to relevant parts of the report at **http://www.official-documents.gov.uk/document/cm23/2370/2370.pdf**. You can also read the CPS Charging Standards at **http://www.cps.gov.uk/legal/l_to_o/offences_against_the_person**. You can find out more about consent by reading, for example, the Law Commission report at **http://onlinelibrary.wiley.com/doi/10.1111/j.1468-2230.1994.tb01984.x/pdf**.

3. **Section A** – be precise in AO1 material and holistic in your AO2. Look beyond the obvious and consider the wider role of the law. Be flexible and respond to the question.

4. **Section B** – be thorough, confident and clear in your application of relevant law to the facts given. Be methodical: make a plan, do not imagine facts and be as decisive as possible.

5. **Section C** – be disciplined, logical and precise. Do not use cases, just their principles.

8 Insanity and automatism

This chapter relates to two key areas:

● insanity/insane automatism

● automatism/non-insane automatism.

Why are insanity and automatism needed?

Revised ☐

● To ensure that defendants who do not have full mental capacity are treated fairly.

● A sign of a civilised legal system.

Insanity/insane automatism

Revised ☐

Definition

● Defendant must be labouring under such a defect of reason, from a disease of the mind, as to not know the nature and quality of the act he was doing or, if he did know it, that he did not know what he was doing was wrong.

Starting point for the defence

● Defendant presumed to be sane.

● Burden of proof rests on defendant to a balance of probabilities.

● Insanity no defence to strict liability crimes.

● Must be evidence from two medical experts.

A defect of reason

● Requires an impairment of reasoning.

● Must be more than being absent minded or confused.

A disease of the mind

● Legal term covering physical and mental conditions.

● Very broad – refers to organic or functional, permanent or transient and intermittent.

● Must be an internal factor and exist at the time the defendant acted.

Not knowing the nature and quality of the act and that legally wrong

- May be due to a state of unconsciousness or impaired consciousness.
- May be due to a lack of understanding or awareness due to a mental condition while conscious.
- No defence if the defendant knows that what they are doing is legally wrong, even if they have a mental illness.

Consequence of insanity verdict

- Before 1991 this resulted in compulsory detention in a mental hospital.
- Criminal Procedure (Insanity and Unfitness to Plead) Act 1991, now replaced by Domestic Violence, Crime and Victims Act 2004, extends sentencing options to:
  - hospital order
  - supervision order
  - absolute discharge
  - murder – an indefinite hospital order with Home Secretary giving permission for release.

Key cases on insanity

Case name	Summary facts	Element of insanity	Legal point
M'Naghten (1843)	M killed Sir Robert Peel's secretary while suffering from extreme paranoia	Definition	Created test for insanity
DPP v H (1997)	H charged with driving with excess alcohol	Definition	Insanity no defence to crime of strict liability
Clarke (1972)	C took items from supermarket without knowing due to diabetes and depression	Defect of reason	CA quashed C's conviction as needed inability to reason, not just imperfect reasoning
Kemp (1956)	K had hardening of arteries; he attacked wife with hammer	Disease of mind	CA upheld insanity as physical illness removed K's mind and ability to reason
Sullivan (1984)	S was an epileptic who injured elderly neighbour during fit when visiting	Disease of mind	HL created broad definition of disease of the mind; source of disease irrelevant
Hennessy (1983)	H diabetic and took no insulin for three days. Charged with taking motor vehicle without consent and driving while disqualified	Disease of mind	CA held insanity correct defence as internal factor affected H's mind
Quick (1973)	Q was a diabetic nurse who took insulin but ate insufficient food and assaulted patient	Disease of mind	CA held condition induced by insulin, an external factor, and insanity not appropriate
Burgess (1991)	B attacked girlfriend after falling asleep watching film	Disease of mind	CA upheld sleep disorder causing sleepwalking as insanity
Windle (1952)	W killed wife with 100 aspirin and said, 'I suppose they will hang me for this'	Wrongness of act	W not insane as knew act wrong in law
Johnson (2007)	J was a paranoid schizophrenic who attacked neighbour	Wrongness of act	J not insane as knew what he was doing and that it was legally wrong

Reform proposals for insanity

- 1953 Royal Commission on Capital Punishment – insanity should be extended to cover those who were incapable of preventing themselves committing an offence.

- 1957 Homicide Act – created defence of diminished responsibility.

- 1975 Butler Committee – recommended verdict of not guilty by evidence of mental disorder.

- 1989 Law Commission Draft Criminal Code Clause 35 – proposed mental disorder verdict based on evidence of severe mental illness or handicap.

- 1991 Criminal Procedure (Insanity and Unfitness to plead) Act, now replaced by Domestic Violence, Crime and Victims Act 2004 – widened sentencing options after insanity verdict.

- 2012 Law Commission scoping paper.

Check your understanding

1. When were the insanity rules created and why is this important?
2. When, and how, were sentencing options changed for insanity?
3. How would the Law Commission redefine insanity?
4. Why is *Sullivan (1984)* such an important case?
5. Consider the case of *Windle (1952)* and make one argument to say that the decision is fair and one to say that it is unfair.

Automatism/non-insane automatism
Revised

Definition

- Act done by the muscles without any control by the mind, such as a spasm, a reflex action or a convulsion; or an act done by a person who is not conscious of what he is doing such as an act done while suffering from concussion or while sleepwalking.

- Based on defendant having no control over their movements and no *mens rea*.

- If successful, leads to acquittal.

There must be an external factor

- Essential if the defendant is to be without fault – in *Kay v Butterworth (1945)* the judge gave examples of what might constitute automatic conduct, such as being struck by a stone, overcome by a sudden illness or a temporary loss of control due to a radical event such as a swarm of bees.

- Role of stress is troublesome for the courts.

There must be a loss of control

- Loss of control must be total.

The automatism must not be self-induced

- No automatism if the defendant knows his conduct is likely to bring on an automatic state.

- If the automatism is self-induced and relates to an offence of specific intent the defence may be available, but for a basic intent offence the necessary *mens rea* is provided by being reckless in managing a condition which can lead to automatism.
- Exception occurs where the defendant does not know his act could lead to an automatic state and he has not been reckless.

Reform proposals for automatism   Revised

- 1989 Draft Criminal Code Clause 33 – automatism will be available when:
  - there was a reflex action, spasm or convulsion
  - a condition, whether of sleep, unconsciousness or otherwise, leads to deprivation of effective control occurring
  - there was an act or condition as a result of nothing done or omitted with the fault required for the offence, or intoxication.

Key cases on automatism

Case name	Summary facts	Element of automatism	Legal point
Bratty (1963)	B strangled girlfriend with stocking whilst having black-out	Definition	Lord Denning created test
Hill v Baxter (1958)	B hit car when failed to stop at junction and said remembered nothing	Need for external factor	Divisional Court QBD directed conviction as no evidence of automatic conduct
Rabey (1980)	R attacked girl due to stress caused by his rejected advances	External factor – stress	Not automatism, but stress of rejection could be insanity
T (1990)	T took part in robbery and assault three days after rape in dream-like state and suffering PTSD	External factor – stress	External stress can give rise to defence if sufficiently severe
Narborough (2004)	N stabbed man. N said flashbacks and PTSD due to childhood sexual abuse meant acted like 'zombie'	External factor – stress	Stress not seen as giving rise to automatism
Isitt (1978)	I drove off after accident, avoiding police car and road block	Total loss of control	No automatism as some control even though evidence of dissociative state
AG Ref (No 2 of 1992) (1993)	Lorry driver drove along motorway hard shoulder and killed two people, but said was in trance-like state	Total loss of control	CA held not automatism as only partial loss of control
Bailey (1983)	B diabetic and taken insulin but not eaten enough before hitting person with iron bar	Self-induced automatism	CA upheld B's conviction as state self-induced
Hardie (1984)	H was depressed and took some of girlfriend's Valium tablets before setting fire to wardrobe. H said no recollection of act	Self-induced automatism	CA quashed H's conviction as normal effect of Valium was tranquiliser so H not reckless

Points for an essay on insanity and automatism

- Insanity:
  - Based on 1843 definition when knowledge of mental illness was basic.
  - Changes to sentencing are helpful but do not address how the defence is put together.

- Legal nature means those who have irresistible impulses or are psychopaths suffering from a recognised mental disorder cannot use it.
- Some physical illnesses are classed as insanity even though relatively common and would not be considered as insanity by ordinary people, creating an uncomfortably fine line, especially for diabetics and epileptics.
- Not available to those who have a mental illness and do not see their act as morally wrong but know their act was wrong in law; the definition of 'wrong' is very narrow and can exclude those to whom the defence should apply.
- Reform proposals would remove any reference to 'wrong' if adopted.
- Those charged with murder usually prefer diminished responsibility as this is broader, often raised successfully and has fewer negative connotations.
- Negative social stigma means many who should have access do not use it; consequently some people receive no treatment and society is unprotected.
- Placing the burden of proof on the defendant may contravene ECHR Article 6.
- Requiring a jury to decide is inappropriate as they do not have medical knowledge and may be affected by the relative performance of medical experts.
- The crime committed may mean that a defendant is deprived of the defence because of a jury's moral revulsion.
- Automatism:
  - Thin dividing line with insanity means cases turn on their facts, leading to uncertainty and inconsistency.
  - Many denied access to the defence, even though they would seem to fall within it, according to the views of ordinary people.
  - Other countries have developed the defence differently: Australia defines insanity as the reaction of an unsound mind to its own delusions or external stimuli, and automatism as the reaction of a sound mind to external stimuli including stress-producing factors.

Check your understanding

6. Give a simple definition of automatism.
7. What is the importance of *T (1990)*?
8. Explain briefly the overlap between automatism and intoxication.
9. What is the importance of cases like *Isitt (1978)*?
10. What impact would proposals for change have on sleepwalkers?

Now test yourself

Tested

1. Look at the chart and decide on the most appropriate defence in each of the situations described.

Act	Insanity or automatism
Sanjay asks Misha to go out with him. She refuses so he asks again. She refuses again. Sanjay sees Misha in the street with another boy and runs up to her, hitting her with a cricket bat he is carrying and shouting, 'If I can't have you, neither can he!'	
Trevor is a teacher and a diabetic. He is late for class and does not have time to take his insulin. During the class Trevor grabs Carly by the throat and she faints. Trevor says he can remember nothing.	
Vincent is a diabetic and he has taken his insulin but did not have time for lunch. Trevor drives home and crashes into a parked car. He recalls nothing but calls the police the next morning when he sees that his car has been damaged by the crash.	

(Continued)

(Continued)

Act	Insanity or automatism
Xavier's sister has been prescribed tranquilisers for her depression. Xavier has had a big argument with his mother and he is so angry he takes some of his sister's tranquilisers to help him calm down. The tranquilisers make Xavier hyperactive and he smashes two windows and a coffee table before falling asleep.	
Benedict invites a friend to watch a film with him. Benedict attacks his friend and says he was sleepwalking.	

2. Copy the table below and fill in the details to test your knowledge. Then make a revision chart with the cases grouped appropriately.

Case name	Factual key words	Insanity or automatism element	Legal importance
T (1990)			
Kemp (1956)			
Quick (1973)			
Hardie (1984)			
AG Ref (No 2 of 1992) (1993)			
Sullivan (1984)			
Hill v Baxter (1958)			
Bratty (1963)			
Bailey (1983)			
M'Naghten (1843)			
Burgess (1991)			
Rabey (1980)			
Clarke (1972)			
Narborough (2004)			
Johnson (2007)			
DPP v H (1997)			
Windle (1952)			
Isitt (1978)			
Hennessy (1983)			

Exam practice – Section A question

Discuss whether the rules governing insanity as a defence in criminal law are in a satisfactory state or are in need of reform.

(Essay question – AO1, AO2, AO3 – 50 marks.)

Check your answers at **www.therevisionbutton.co.uk/myrevisionnotes**

Online

Exam summary

✔ These defences can appear anywhere on the paper so be sure you can explain the similarities and differences between them clearly.

✔ **Section A** – there is a lot of AO2 so good structure is important.

✔ **Section B** – read the question carefully to gauge how much detail is needed. Some **Section B** questions focus on defences so your knowledge must be thorough.

✔ **Section C** – read the statement carefully and apply the principles of the correct defence.

Striving for an A/A*?

1. Take your research further, for example, you can read about common conditions that the law may treat as insanity at **http://www.epilepsy.org.uk** and **http://www.diabetes.org.uk**. You can check on the Law Commission's latest ideas at **http://lawcommission.justice.gov.uk/areas/insanity.htm**.

2. **Section A** – consider wider issues relating to defences which deal with mental capacity and make links to other areas such as diminished responsibility.

3. **Section B** – use cases appropriately and be confident when identifying, explaining and applying different kinds of conditions, especially diabetes.

4. **Section C** – be logical, concise and precise. Be sure to reach a conclusion.

9 Duress and necessity

This chapter relates to three key areas:

- duress by threats
- duress of circumstances
- necessity.

Duress Revised

- The defendant is forced to commit a crime because a threat of death or serious harm effectively deprives them of a choice whether to act.

Why is there a defence of duress?

- To prevent a person being guilty of a crime they would never otherwise commit.

Is duress a defence to all crimes?

- No – there is no defence to murder, attempted murder and, possibly, treason.
- This applies to principal or secondary offenders.

Duress by threats Revised

Definition

- A person's will is overborne by threats so that he commits an act he would not otherwise do.

How serious must the threat be?

- Threat must be of death or serious injury.
- Can be a combination of threats but those of death or serious injury must play a part.

Who must be threatened?

- Defendant, family members and even a passenger in a car have given rise to the defence.

The Graham (1982) test

- Was the defendant compelled to act because he reasonably believed he had good reason to fear death or serious injury; and
- Would a sober person of reasonable firmness, sharing the same characteristics as the defendant, have acted in the same way?

Example

In *Martin (DP) (2000)* M suffered from a schizoid-affective disorder which meant he could perceive things said to him as a threat that would be carried out. He relied on this when claiming to have been forced to carry out two robberies. The trial judge said M's disorder was only relevant to the second part of the *Graham* test. M appealed, saying that the jury should have considered whether in view of his condition he may have reasonably feared for his safety. The CA quashed his conviction and said that the same principles should apply as in self-defence where an honestly held belief gives rise to the defence, even if it is mistaken and unreasonable, but in *Hasan (2005)* the court appeared to revert to the traditional view expressed in *Graham*.

While the first element of the *Graham* test is somewhat subjective, the second is objective, as only some characteristics are relevant, including age, pregnancy, a serious physical disability, gender and a recognised mental illness or psychiatric disorder.

What if there is a safe avenue of escape?

- This negates the defence.
- In exceptional situations the defence might still be available.

When must the threat occur?

- Must be effective and operate on the defendant when the crime is committed.
- Must be imminent peril of death or serious injury to the defendant or to those for whom he has responsibility.

What must be threatened?

- Nexus – a threat to commit a particular offence.

What if the belief in a threat comes as a result of intoxication?

- A mistake due to voluntarily intoxication negates the defence.
- If there is no mistake and the intoxication does not affect whether there is duress or not the defence can still succeed.

What if the duress is self-induced?

- Usually this negates the defence.
- The courts have shown some flexibility.

Key cases on duress by threats

Case name	Summary facts	Element of duress	Legal point
Howe (1987)	H was one of a group who abused and killed a man. On later occasion H abused and killed a man. H said he acted because he had been threatened	Availability	HL refused H defence of duress as no life worth more than another
Wilson (2007)	W, aged 13, and father accused of mother's murder. W said scared to disobey father	Availability	W no defence
Gotts (1992)	G, aged 16, threatened with violence by father so stabbed mother	Availability	G no duress to attempted murder
Valderrama-Vega (1985)	V imported cocaine and said received threats of death, financial ruin and exposure of homosexuality	Type of threat	CA said all threats considered as death threatened
Wright (2000)	W arrested with cocaine and said acted because boyfriend threatened	Person threatened	Person subject to threat extended beyond immediate family

(Continued)

(Continued)

Case name	Summary facts	Element of duress	Legal point
Graham (1982)	G was homosexual who lived with wife and K. G helped K kill wife and said acted as scared of K	Test	CA created standard test
Bowen (1996)	B, IQ of 68, obtained goods by deception for men who threatened to petrol-bomb B and family	Test	B's IQ not relevant characteristic as not part of ability to resist pressure and threats
Gill (1963)	G claimed he and wife been threatened unless he stole lorry	Safe avenue of escape	No defence as G could have reported threat in time lapse before theft
Hudson and Taylor (1971)	H and T were teenage girls who gave perjured evidence because threatened with having faces cut	Safe avenue of escape	CA quashed convictions as could have sought police protection but not realistic for them
Abdul-Hussain (1999)	A and others hijacked plane which landed in UK as feared return to Iraq	Immediacy/ imminence	CA overturned convictions, threat need only be imminent
Cole (1994)	C robbed building societies to repay debt as he and family threatened	Nexus	C's conviction upheld as no nexus between threat and offence
Sharp (1987)	S joined robbery gang, tried to leave before sub-postmaster killed in robbery	Self-induced duress	S no defence as knew gang likely to use violence
Shepherd (1987)	S joined shoplifting gang, threatened with violence when tried to leave	Self-induced duress	S conviction quashed as S no knowledge gang likely to use violence
Heath (2000)	H owed money to drug dealer and threatened so supplied cannabis	Self-induced duress	H no defence as knew getting into debt with drug dealer meant threat of violence existed
Hasan (2005)	H associated with violent drug dealer and told to burgle house and open safe or he and family harmed. H entered house with knife but could not open safe	Self-induced duress / Test	H no defence as association with drug dealer meant foresaw or ought reasonably to have foreseen risk of compulsion by threats of violence

Duress of circumstances · Revised

- The threat comes from circumstances rather than a direct threat.
- The defence has evolved during the last 25 years because of the limits in duress by threats.
- There is a two part test in *Martin (1989)*:
  - was the defendant compelled to act as he did because he reasonably believed he had good reason to fear death or serious injury, and
  - if so, would a sober person of reasonable firmness sharing the characteristics of the accused have acted in the same way?
- Now extends beyond driving offences.
- As in duress by threats, there must be a danger of death or serious injury.
- There is an argument that duress of circumstances is the same as necessity. However, they can also be argued to be separate defences, especially as necessity, but not duress by threats, can be pleaded to a charge of murder.

Necessity · Revised

- Defendant acts to prevent a worse evil happening.
- Has been very difficult to recognise the existence of this defence.
- Methods of avoiding this defence have been used.
- Necessity now exists but remains potentially limited in scope.

- CA has said that duress of circumstances and necessity are effectively the same thing and the test should be:
  - that the act must be done only to prevent an act of greater evil
  - the evil must be directed towards the defendant or a person or persons for whom he has responsibility
  - the act must be reasonable and proportionate to the evil.
- Necessity can apply in relation to self-defence.
- Necessity can also apply in relation to s5(2)(b) Criminal Damage Act 1971 where it is a defence to say that other property was at risk and in need of immediate protection, as long as the defendant acted reasonably.

Example

In *Buckoke v GLC (1971)* Lord Denning's *obiter dicta* suggested that although a member of the emergency services might not be able to run a defence of necessity in an extreme situation, they would in fact be congratulated and the discretion to prosecute should be used to ensure they did not appear in court.

Key cases on duress of circumstances and necessity

Case name	Summary facts	Element of defence	Legal point
Willer (1986)	W and passenger in car surrounded by threatening youths. W drove slowly on pavement to escape	Beginnings of duress of circumstances	CA said jury should be able to consider whether W drove under some kind of duress
Conway (1988)	C's passenger saw men and thought they had shot at him so C drove off fast	Beginnings of duress of circumstances	CA quashed C's conviction saying duress possible defence if from objective perspective acting to avoid threat of death or serious injury
Martin (1989)	M's wife threatened suicide unless M drove son to work. M had lost licence	Test for duress of circumstances	CA adapted test from *Graham (1982)*
Pommell (1995)	P found by police with gun in bed during drugs raid. P said taken gun from man and going to hand it in	Extent of defence of duress of circumstances	CA held duress of circumstances could apply to any offence
Cairns (1999)	Man threw himself on to bonnet of C's car. C felt threatened so drove off with man on bonnet. C braked, man fell under car and badly injured	Extent of defence of duress of circumstances	C's conviction quashed as reasonably perceived threat of serious injury or death
Dudley and Stephens (1884)	D and S adrift at sea without food and water and ate cabin boy	Extent of necessity	No defence – no life worth more than another
Re F (1990)	Health authority applied for declaration to sterilise F, a severely mentally disabled woman at risk of pregnancy	Development of necessity	HL granted declaration – lawful duty of doctors to act based on necessity
Re A (2000)	Health authority applied for declaration to separate conjoined twins so one lived but the other died	Development of necessity	Lord Brook applied necessity – act done to avoid otherwise unavoidable consequences which would inflict inevitable and irreparable evil. No more done than reasonably necessary and evil done not disproportionate to that avoided
Shayler (2001)	S past member of MI5 charged with breaching OSA 1989	Limit of necessity and present definition	No defence of necessity and redefined as Lord Woolf used same test as Lord Brook in *Re A*. Suggested duress of circumstances and necessity interchangeable.

Reform proposals for duress and necessity
Revised ☐

- 1993 Law Commission Legislating the Criminal Code: Offences Against the Person and General Principles – duress should be available to all crimes.

- 2005 Law Commission consultation paper A New Homicide Act –
  duress should be a partial defence to murder.
- 2006 Law Commission report Murder, Manslaughter and Infanticide –
  duress should be a defence to murder.

Points for an essay on duress and necessity

- If defences are a concession to human frailty arguably they should mitigate, not excuse.
- Difficult to understand how a defendant was feeling.
- Defences are difficult to raise successfully as they lead to acquittal.
- Lack of duress in murder is based on impractical moral principles of heroism; the human condition dictates survival and protection of loved ones – the Law Commission has proposed change.
- Inconsistent that necessity has been successfully raised for murder.
- Harsh that a defendant's age or susceptibility is irrelevant to duress.
- Harsh that no account taken of IQ as understanding of a threat influences reaction.
- Duress is available for s18 OAPA 1861 which seems inequitable.
- Unhelpful lack of clarity on seeking police protection – some people have no confidence in the police and the police cannot always provide effective protection.
- Policy drives the law, especially in relation to criminals and terrorists.
- Necessity basis in moral Victorian principles has stymied its growth.
- Having to rely on the discretion to prosecute suggests that reform is needed although in some circumstances necessity would now be available.
- Inconsistent as duress requires a threat to a defendant or to someone for whom they feel responsible, whereas necessity is much more broadly drawn.
- Duress of circumstances has seen beneficial development; this is not the same as necessity as the latter defence is available for murder and attempted murder. Extent over overlap unclear, as seen in *Quayle (2005)* and *Altham (2006)*.

Check your understanding

1. Define the test in *Graham (1982)* and explain the basis of each element.
2. What problem is raised by the case of *Wilson (2007)*?
3. Explain two ways in which the defence of duress could be improved by reform.
4. Why is *Re A (2000)* important?
5. What is the problem with relying on the discretion to prosecute in necessity?

Now test yourself

Tested

1. Copy the table below and fill in the details to test your knowledge and then make a revision chart linking the cases to the correct defence.

Case name	Factual key words	Area of defence	Legal importance
Gill (1963)			
Re A (2000)			
Gotts (1992)			

(Continued)

(Continued)

Case name	Factual key words	Area of defence	Legal importance
Cole (1994)			
Pommell (1995)			
Shepherd (1987)			
Martin (1989)			
Howe (1987)			
Dudley and Stephens (1884)			
Graham (1982)			
Re F (1990)			
Wilson (2007)			
Willer (1986)			
Hudson and Taylor (1971)			
Cairns (1999)			
Heath (2000)			
Valderrama-Vega (1985)			
Sharp (1987)			
Wright (2000)			
Bowen (1996)			
Abdul-Hussain (1999)			
Hasan (2005)			

Exam summary

✔ **Section A** – duress and necessity are good topics as there are many AO2 points you can make. You need to be clear in your explanation of the law and analysis needs to be developed so practise this beforehand.

✔ **Section B** – be clear on the elements and read the scenario carefully for any clues to help you apply particular aspects of these defences accurately.

✔ **Section C** – principles are all-important although scenarios are often based on well known cases.

Striving for an A/A*?

1. Take your research further – visit the Law Commission website at **http://lawcommission.justice.gov.uk**.

2. **Section A** – consider the development of these defences, their effectiveness and the policy issues which have been influential. A wider approach helps to make your essay more sophisticated and holistic – qualities which are the sign of a top student.

3. **Section B** – be accurate, confident and clear in your application. Give factual knowledge but balance it with application as you go along.

4. **Section C** – be disciplined, logical, concise, precise and decisive.

10 Intoxication and self-defence

This chapter relates to two key areas:

- intoxication
- self-defence.

Intoxication   Revised ☐

- Defendant cannot form necessary *mens rea* due to intoxication.
- Intoxication can be voluntary or involuntary.

Why can this be a defence?   Revised ☐

- Important to treat defendants fairly if they have no *mens rea*.
- Balanced by a need to send out a strong deterrent message and protect society.

> **Exam tip**
>
> **Section A** – learn definitions carefully and make sure you have the categories of intoxication clear. This helps to reinforce AO2 comment, much of which centres on the balance between legal principle and public policy.
>
> **Section B** and **Section C** – thorough knowledge is also crucial for good application.

> **Typical mistake**
>
> **Section A** – not using the best cases to illustrate AO2 points.
>
> **Section B** and **Section C** – not reading scenarios carefully to pick out the correct type of intoxication and making links to other defences.

Voluntary intoxication   Revised ☐

Definition

- Defendant chooses to take an intoxicating substance.
- Includes drugs, drink or other substances.
- Also includes the taking of a prescribed drug when the defendant knows it will lead to intoxication.

Specific intent offences

- Defendant must be so intoxicated that there is no *mens rea*.
- A drunken intent is still an intent.
- If intoxication is used as Dutch courage there is no defence.
- Liability is normally reduced to that of a lesser included offence.

Basic intent offences

- Intoxication is not a defence.
- Becoming intoxicated provides the *mens rea* needed for the offence.

Involuntary intoxication

Revised

Basic elements

- Defendant does not know they have taken an intoxicating substance.
- Defendant may have taken prescribed drugs which have an unexpected effect.
- No defence if the defendant has the necessary *mens rea* at the time of the offence.
- Lowering of inhibitions through intoxication is no defence if the necessary *mens rea* exists.
- Successfully raising the defence leads to acquittal.

Intoxication and mistake

Revised

- Defence exists if the mistake prevents the defendant having *mens rea* for a specific intent offence.
- No defence if the mistake prevents the defendant having *mens rea* for a basic intent offence.
- s76(5) Criminal Justice and Immigration Act 2008 – a mistaken belief caused through voluntary intoxication cannot give rise to self-defence, defence of another or prevention of crime.
- s5 Criminal Damage Act 1971 – creates a defence based on an honest belief that the person to whom the property belonged would have consented to the damage had they known about it, even where the mistake is induced by intoxication.

Reform proposals for intoxication

Revised

- 1975 Butler Committee – a defence of dangerous intoxication – a defendant could still be convicted of an offence where they had been acquitted of the main offence with which they were charged because of intoxication.
- 1993 Law Commission – intoxication should be relevant to all crimes that needed *mens rea* and the creation of an offence of criminal intoxication.
- 1995 – earlier ideas were dropped and the Law Commission suggested codifying the existing law with a few amendments.
- 2009 Law Commission Report Intoxication and Criminal Liability (Law Com 314) recommendations:
  - Retain distinction between specific and basic intent crimes but replace with offences where *mens rea* is an integral fault element and those where it is not.
  - Create general rule that where the defendant is charged with an offence for which *mens rea* is not an integral fault element then he should be treated as being aware of anything he would have been aware of if he had been sober.
  - No application to offences where required *mens rea* involved intention as to a consequence, knowledge, fraud or dishonesty.

- Drawing up a list of conditions giving rise to involuntary intoxication – having a drink spiked, being drugged or where intoxication results from taking drugs for a proper medical purpose – and taking these into account to decide on *mens rea*.

Key cases on intoxication

Case name	Summary facts	Element of intoxication	Legal point
Beard (1920)	B raised intoxication to murder charge	Definition	Lord Birkenhead said B must be incapable of forming *mens rea* necessary for offence
Sheehan and Moore (1975)	S and M killed tramp when very drunk and set fire to him	Definition	S and M not convicted of murder as no *mens rea* due to intoxication but convicted of manslaughter
AG for Northern Ireland v Gallagher (1963)	G decided to kill wife, so bought whisky and knife. G drank some whisky before killing wife	Definition – Dutch courage	G's conviction for murder upheld as *mens rea* formed before intoxication
DPP v Majewski (1977)	M extremely intoxicated and attacked pub, people in it and police arresting him	Recklessness and intoxication	s47 OAPA 1861 and assaulting police officer in execution of duty upheld by HL as M's recklessness result of intoxication
Kingston (1994)	K, a known paedophile, given drugged coffee by blackmailer and photographed abusing sleeping teenage boy	Extent of involuntary intoxication	HL upheld K's conviction as had *mens rea* for offence
Hardie (1984)	H depressed and took some of girlfriend's Valium tablets before setting fire to wardrobe	Involuntary intoxication	CA quashed H's conviction as normal effect of Valium tranquiliser, so H not reckless and no *mens rea*
Lipman (1970)	L and girlfriend took LSD and fell asleep. When L woke had killed girlfriend mistaking her for snake	Mistake and intoxication	L guilty of manslaughter, not murder, as taken LSD voluntarily
O'Grady (1987)	O and friend drinking heavily and fell asleep. O said woke to find being hit so hit friend with glass ashtray. Next morning friend dead	Mistake and intoxication / Self-defence	O convicted of manslaughter as intoxication no defence for crime of basic intent
Hatton (2005)	H very drunk and went back to flat with man. Next morning man dead with sledgehammer injuries. H said remembered defending self against attack	Mistake and intoxication / Self-defence	H conviction upheld. CA said drunken mistake as to force needed in self-defence no defence to crimes of basic or specific intent
Jaggard v Dickinson (1980)	D drunk and went to friend's house but out so D broke window to enter as believed friend would consent to this. D broke into wrong house	Mistake and intoxication	D's conviction quashed by Divisional Court QBD based on s5 CDA 1971

Points for an essay on intoxication

- Largely driven by public policy; there is a fine line between need to recognise lack of full control at the time of the offence and strong deterrent message about using intoxicating substances.

- Dilemma is intensified as around 50 per cent of crimes involve intoxication and many prisoners have alcohol and drug dependency problems.

- Public policy often prevails over the legal principle that a person not in control and not able to form *mens rea* should not be convicted.

- Convictions facilitated through the continuing act theory – there can be a considerable time delay between becoming intoxicated and committing an offence.

- Although a defendant may be reckless in becoming intoxicated, they often have no thought of committing any offence, much less a particular offence, and so conviction seems to go against basic principles.

- Fall-back is often a way out but for some offences, such as theft, this option is not available.

- Involuntary intoxication is a difficult defence to achieve and goes against legal principle, as the defendant was not to blame for their intoxicated state. It seems harsh to punish a person whose self-control to resist even anti-social and criminal tendencies is taken away by a third party.
- Arguably it would be more effective to create an offence of becoming intoxicated.
- However, there are practical influences as alcohol sales raise considerable revenue for the government and there are some suggested health benefits to consuming alcohol in moderation; contrasts with policing and NHS costs alongside government's agenda to counter anti-social behaviour.

Check your understanding

1. How does the law deal with Dutch courage and why does it take this position?
2. What is the importance of the decision in *Majewski (1977)*?
3. Why is *Jaggard v Dickinson (1988)* important?
4. Explain what fall-back means in the defence of intoxication.
5. What is the significance of *Hatton (2005)*?

Self-defence, defence of another and prevention of crime

Revised

- Self-defence and defence of another found in common law.
- s3(1) Criminal Law Act 1967 – statutory defence of prevention of crime – a person may use force reasonable in the circumstances to prevent crime or arrest or help to arrest offenders, suspected offenders or persons unlawfully at large.
- Criminal Justice and Immigration Act 2008 clarifies the law.

Exam tip

Learn definitions thoroughly, alongside relevant case citation. Have some comment ready as this topic can appear in **Section A** and is often an aspect of **Section B** and **Section C**.

Typical mistake

It is easy to get confused with the elements of this defence, especially as it overlaps with other areas, so be sure to make this a key part of your revision.

Why can this be a defence?

Revised

- Defence is essential for those in a situation where they do things they never normally would.
- Tightly drawn to protect society and vital not to give excuse for violence.

Elements of the defence

Revised

What degree of force is acceptable?

- Criminal Justice and Immigration Act 2008 – difficult for a person to weigh up exactly how much force is needed in a pressure situation, so assessed by what they honestly and instinctively thought was reasonable, although the force must be used when the danger of the situation is still on-going.
- Subjective test.
- No duty to retreat.

What if a mistake is made about the level of force needed?

- Defendant is judged by the circumstances as he honestly believed them to be.
- Jury decides if amount of force used was reasonable, based on defendant's genuine perception.
- s76(3) CJIA 2008 confirms a mistake need only be honest and not necessarily reasonable.

What if the mistake is as a result of intoxication?

- Drunken mistake is no defence.

What if the defendant uses a pre-emptive strike?

- Defendant can act first to prevent force.
- Sometimes defendant can take precautions, and even break the law, so he can defend himself should the need arise.

What if the defendant uses excessive force?

- The defence will fail.

Are the defendant's characteristics relevant?

- Characteristics are not relevant to whether the defendant used reasonable force.
- s76 CJIA 2008 – casts doubt on this principle as it does not make mention of exclusions based on psychiatric conditions and so the presumption is that they will be taken into account in future cases.
- s54 Coroners and Justice Act 2009 – provides a defence if self-control is lost due to a fear of serious violence if a person of the defendant's age and sex with a normal degree of tolerance and self-restraint and in the circumstances of the defendant might have reacted in the same or a similar way.

Key cases on self-defence

Case name	Summary facts	Element of self-defence	Legal point
Bird (1985)	B gouged out ex-boyfriend's eye during heated argument and after he hit B	Duty to retreat	B's conviction quashed as evidence of retreat helpful but not essential
Williams (1987)	W grabbed and injured police officer mistakenly thought was assaulting youth	Type of mistake needed	CA quashed W's assault conviction as jury had been directed mistake to be reasonable but it need only be honest
AG Reference (No 2 of 1983) (1984)	Man's shop was attacked during riots so he made and stored petrol bombs for protection	Possibility of pre-emptive action	CA held could make preparations in self-defence
Clegg (1995)	C was soldier on check-point duty who fired bullets at passing car mistakenly, thinking it was terrorists, but last bullet killed joy-rider	Excessive force	C no self-defence as final bullet excessive force
Martin (Anthony) (2002)	M shot and killed burglar as ran away and wounded other	Excessive force Relevant characteristics	M no self-defence, firing at person running away. Excessive force although had psychiatric condition and perceived greater danger than average person

Points for an essay on self-defence

- Difficult for a jury to put themselves in the shoes of the defendant to decide if force was necessary.
- All-or-nothing defences can be difficult for juries.
- The defence embodies competing moral principles.
- There is a need to ensure that vigilante justice is not legitimised or encouraged.
- There are inconsistencies in deciding whether something is a pre-emptive strike.
- Relevance, or otherwise, of psychiatric conditions is confusing and it is debatable whether someone feeling vulnerable can be expected to use only reasonable force.
- New links to loss of self-control are provided by s54 Coroners and Justice Act 2009 but largely untested.
- On-going controversial discussion about householder rights of self-defence.
- Self-defence can be useful, for example as the rationale behind Lord Justice Ward's thinking in *Re A (2000)*.
- There is a danger of a two-tier defence if citizens and those with public duties are treated differently.
- Is it right to require a mistake to be one the defendant would have made if sober when intoxication is probably the reason why the defendant is upset and confused?

Check your understanding

6. How did the case of *Bird (1985)* change the law?
7. How is the defence affected if excessive force is used?
8. Explain how the test relating to a mistaken need for force works.
9. Which statute is the most recent with regard to self-defence?
10. Why should self-defence be a defence and give two problems with this defence.

Now test yourself

Tested ☐

1. Look at the chart and decide on the most appropriate defence in each of the situations described. Comment on whether the defence is likely to be successful.

	Intoxication or self-defence	Reasoning
Yuri wants to kills his father so he can inherit his money. Yuri drinks a bottle of vodka and then stabs his father with a knife.		
Eric has been on a night out and climbs into the house he rents by breaking a small window as the landlord has told him this is okay. When Eric gets inside he realises he has broken into the house next door.		
Anya has been to a party to celebrate her new job. She drinks only orange juice but is stopped and breathalysed by the police after she is seen driving the wrong way round a roundabout. Anya is over the limit because her friends put vodka in her orange juice.		
Rupert has been drinking all day to celebrate his A Level results. As he is going home Rupert is approached by a man. The man is going to ask Rupert for money but Rupert thinks he is about to be attacked and punches the man so hard his nose is broken.		
Sasha is a heroin addict. Her dealer demands more money for the heroin he sells her. Sasha pays the dealer but she is so angry she follows him down the street and hits him from behind with a brick. The dealer dies.		

2. Copy the table below and for each of the cases, insert key words that show you have matched the correct case to its name. Then summarise why the case is important.

Case name	Factual key words	Area of law	Legal importance
Bird (1985)			
Beard (1920)			

(Continued)

(Continued)

Case name	Factual key words	Area of law	Legal importance
Williams (1987)			
Kingston (1994)			
AG Ref (No 2 of 1983) (1984)			
O'Grady (1987)			
Gallagher (1963)			
Clegg (1995)			
Jaggard v Dickinson (1980)			
Majewski (1977)			
Martin (Anthony) (2002)			
Hatton (2005)			
Hardie (1984)			
Sheehan and Moore (1975)			
Lipman (1970)			

3. Make a revision mind map sorting cases into their correct defence categories.

Exam practice – Section B question

Maya and Christina decide to go out for the night. They meet at Christina's house and begin the evening by drinking several glasses of gin. When they arrive at a pub, Christina orders drinks. The barman, Shaun, asks them for proof of age and Maya, who thinks Shaun is insulting them, picks up a glass of lager from the bar and throws the contents in Shaun's face. When Terry, another customer, steps forward to intervene, Christina mistakenly thinks he is going to grab Maya so she picks up another glass and smashes it into Terry's face, gouging out his eye.

Discuss the offences which Maya and Christina may have committed and any potential defences open to them.

(Hypothetical problem/case study question – AO1, AO2, AO3 – 50 marks.)

Check your answers at **www.therevisionbutton.co.uk/myrevisionnotes**

Online

Exam summary

✔ These defences may appear in any section of the exam paper so you need to be well prepared.

✔ **Section A** – there could be an essay on either topic; there is some overlap between them, as with automatism and defences in the Coroners and Justice Act 2009, so be well organised with your factual and analytical material.

✔ **Section B** – these defences may well appear as a component in a larger question. Be alert to the scenario facts and be guided by them with regard to how much detail you need to include and the elements of the defences which are relevant. Resist the temptation to write about everything!

✔ **Section C** – apply the principles of the defences concisely and accurately.

Striving for an A/A*?

1. Take your research for an essay further and investigate the wider role of these defences. For example, look at s54 Coroners and Justice Act 2009 and then consider its implications at **http://www.legislation.gov.uk/ukpga/2009/25/section/54**. You can also look in more detail at s76 CJIA 2008 at **http://www.legislation.gov.uk/ukpga/2008/4/section/76**.

2. Use past paper questions to practise spotting where the defences in this chapter would be relevant.

11 Theft

- This chapter relates to sections 1–7 Theft Act 1968.

What is theft in law?

Revised ☐

- s1 – the dishonest appropriation of property belonging to another with the intention of permanently depriving the other of it.
- s1 is the only charge.
- s2–6 define the elements.
- s7 – triable either way offence, with a maximum penalty of seven years.

Why is there a law on theft?

Revised ☐

- Common area of conflict and criminal activity.
- Need to punish those who break the law and send out a strong deterrent message.

Appropriation – s3

Revised ☐

- 's3(1) – any assumption by a person of the rights of an owner amounts to an appropriation, and this includes, where he has come by the property (innocently or not) without stealing it, any later assumption of a right to it by keeping or dealing with it as owner.'

What is an appropriation?

- Must be an act which assumes at least one of the owner's rights.

What about consent?

- Can be an appropriation with the consent of the owner.
- Emphasis is now placed on defendant's *mens rea*.

What if the defendant is given the property?

- Can be an appropriation even when property is a valid gift in civil law.

Appropriation as a continuing act

- Appropriation is not a continuing act.

A later assumption of a right

- Even if property is acquired lawfully appropriation occurs when a defendant does something with the property that assumes any of the owner's rights.

Property – s4 ———————————————————————————— Revised ☐

What is property?

- Money – coins and banknotes of any currency.
- Personal property – covers all moveable items.
- Real property – under s4(2) land can be stolen when a trustee or personal representative takes land in breach of his duties as a trustee, someone not in possession of land severs something forming part of the land from it, and when a tenant takes a fixture or structure from the land let to him.
- Things in action – includes bank accounts and cheques.
- Other intangible property – includes patents but not information.
- Mushrooms, flowers, fruit or foliage – under s4(3) it is possible to steal cultivated examples of these things and also ones which belong to someone. Wild examples of these things can be stolen if they are intended to be sold for commercial reward.
- Animals – under s4(4) it is theft if an animal ordinarily kept in captivity is stolen.

Belonging to another – s5 ———————————————————— Revised ☐

Ownership, possession or control

- Any one element is sufficient.
- Possession or control does not need to be lawful.
- Possible to possess or control property which is not known to be there.
- Charitable donations can sometimes be stolen.
- A proprietary interest in property does not necessarily mean a person cannot steal the property.
- A person can commit theft even if they own property if another person has a proprietary interest in it.

Property received under an obligation

- s5(3) – can still be theft if there is an obligation to deal with property in a particular way.
- s5(4) – where money is received by mistake and without an obligation to return it would no longer be property belonging to another for the purposes of theft.
- Must be a legal obligation to return property.

Key cases on *actus reus* of theft

Case name	Summary facts	Element of theft	Legal point
Pitham and Hehl (1977)	Selling furniture belonging to another person	Appropriation – s3	Appropriation existed and no need to remove furniture
Morris (1983)	M swapped price labels on two products and placed lower priced product in shopping basket	Appropriation – s3	Appropriation was any interference with any of owner's rights. Lord Roskill *obiter dicta* said appropriation should be act done without owner's consent
Lawrence (1972)	L took money from wallet offered by Italian student	Appropriation – s3	Appropriation as student only consented to proper amount of money being taken
Gomez (1993)	G assistant manager of shop who persuaded boss to sell goods. G paid with stolen cheques	Appropriation – s3	CA quashed G's conviction but restored by HL as appropriation could occur with consent
Hinks (2000)	H befriended naïve man who gave H about £60,000 and television	Appropriation – s3	Appropriation existed even though money was legal gift in civil law
Atakpu and Abrahams (1994)	A and A hired luxury cars in EU using false documentation and brought cars to UK	Appropriation – s3	No appropriation as occurred outside UK jurisdiction and not continuing act
Kelly and Lindsay (1998)	K made sculpture casts of body parts L brought from job at Royal College of Surgeons	Property – s4	CA held body parts had been changed and became property
Oxford v Moss (1979)	Student copied proof of examination paper	Property – s4	Information on paper not property
Woodman (1974)	W took scrap metal from property belonging to English China Clays	Belonging to another – s5	W convicted even though ECC did not know scrap metal existed
Turner (No 2) (1971)	T left car at garage for repairs and took it back using spare key without paying bill	Belonging to another – s5	T convicted, even as owner, as car in possession and control of garage
R (on the application of Ricketts) v Basildon Magistrates' Court (2010)	R took bags from outside charity shop, claiming been abandoned, and took bags from bin behind charity shop	Belonging to another – s5	Bags outside shop belonged to donor; those in bin behind shop were property of shop
Webster (2006)	W sold medal when mistakenly sent two by MOD after service in Iraq	Belonging to another – s5	W convicted as MOD retained proprietary interest in medal
Hall (1972)	H was travel agent who placed travel deposits in general bank account and business failed	Belonging to another – s5(3)	H conviction quashed as no obligation to use each deposit to buy particular tickets
Klineberg and Marsden (1999)	K and M ran timeshare company. Purchasers told money going into independent trust company but most went straight to K and M	Belonging to another – s5(3)	K and M convicted of theft as obligation to deal with money in particular way
Davidge v Bunnett (1984)	B given money by flatmates to pay bills but bought Christmas presents	Belonging to another – s5(3)	B convicted of theft as obligation to deal with money in particular way
AG Reference (No 1 of 1983) (1985)	Woman mistakenly overpaid salary by £74.74 into her bank account	Belonging to another – s5(4)	CA said obligation to restore money and when dishonest intention not to restore theft was complete
Gilks (1972)	G mistakenly overpaid by bookmaker but kept money	Belonging to another – s5(4)	No theft as betting transactions not legally enforceable

Dishonesty – s2 — Revised ☐

- Motive is irrelevant.

What is not dishonest?

- s2(1)(a) – honest belief in a legal right to deprive the other person of property.
- s2(1)(b) – honest belief that the owner would consent.
- s2(1)(c) – honest belief that the owner cannot be found, having taken reasonable steps to do so.
- A willingness to pay does not prevent a conviction for theft, even where a defendant takes something and leaves money which is greater than the value of the property to pay for it.

Dishonesty using the Ghosh test

- Used when s2 exceptions do not apply and a common sense definition is insufficient for the jury.
- Was the defendant dishonest according to the ordinary standards of reasonable and honest people? This is an objective element.
- Did the defendant realise he was dishonest by those standards? This is both subjective and objective.

Example

In *Ghosh (1982)* G was a locum doctor who claimed fees for an operation he had not done and said he was not dishonest as he was owed the same amount in consultation fees. He appealed against his conviction and the CA created a new test.

Intention to permanently deprive – s6 — Revised ☐

- Given a broad interpretation, for example, where money taken and the same value replaced with different notes or coins.
- Destruction of property amounts to a permanent deprivation.
- If the person who takes the property uses it as his own, regardless of the owner's rights, this falls within s6.
- Borrowing can be theft if it is equivalent to an outright taking or disposal which means that for all practical purposes the value, or a significant proportion of the value, has gone from the property even if there is an intention to return the property.
- Conditional intent is sufficient where the defendant will steal if there is something worth taking.

Key cases on *mens rea* of theft

Case name	Summary facts	Element of theft	Legal point
Holden (1991)	H took tyres home from work as seen others do it and believed to be perk of job	Dishonesty – s2(1)(a)	H not convicted as had honest belief in legal right
Small (1998)	S drove car which had not moved for week but was unlocked with key in ignition	Dishonesty – s2(1)(c)	S not convicted as honest belief car had been abandoned

(Continued)

(Continued)

Case name	Summary facts	Element of theft	Legal point
DPP v Gohill and another (2007)	G and another were manager and assistant manager of business hiring equipment and changed computer records so some customers paid less	Dishonesty – *Ghosh*	Divisional Court QBD held conduct was within the *Ghosh* test and sent case back for retrial
Velumyl (1989)	V was a manager who took money from office safe, intending to return it when repaid money owed	Intention to permanently deprive – s6	CA upheld V conviction as intended to permanently deprive company of particular notes; intention to replace with different notes irrelevant
Lavender (1994)	L took doors from council property being repaired and used them	Intention to permanently deprive – s6	L's conviction upheld as council had proprietary interest in doors and L treated them as if his own
Lloyd (1985)	L lent film by cinema projectionist friend, made copy overnight and returned film	Intention to permanently deprive – s6	No theft as film returned in original state and no intention to permanently deprive
Easom (1971)	E picked up handbag in cinema and looked inside but replaced it, taking nothing	Intention to permanently deprive – s6	E's theft conviction quashed as no evidence intended to permanently deprive owner of bag or contents

Points for an essay

- *Actus reus*:
  - Appropriation:
    - Broad definition is not necessarily what Parliament intended.
    - Not a continuing act – inconsistent with robbery and burglary.
    - Unintended consequence is that an honest shopper appropriates when taking an item off a shelf.
    - Gifts create uneasy conflict between civil and criminal law.
    - Broad definition pushes situations into s1 which fit better elsewhere, for example s15.
    - Breadth of appropriation puts huge emphasis on dishonesty, with *mens rea* notoriously hard to prove.
    - Problematic to have a key element of such a common offence possibly still open to debate.
  - Property:
    - Also defined broadly but this is often helpful.
  - Belonging to another:
    - Defined widely which can be helpful, although strange that a person can steal their own property.
- *Mens rea*:
  - Dishonesty:
    - Now a key discriminator in theft, but problematic, as explained by Professor Griew and described in the points below.
    - It leaves a lot to the jury which can lead to inconsistency.
    - The objective element in the *Ghosh* test is overly significant.
    - A lacuna means that a defendant escapes conviction if he was dishonest and intended to be so, but the ordinary man does not share that view or he honestly believes no reasonable person would see his conduct as dishonest.
    - Trials are longer as there is more to explain to the jury.
    - Trials are more complex as this is a difficult concept for a jury.
    - People do not all have the same standards of dishonesty – this is borne out by the Law Commission and 2009 research by Finch and Fafinsky.
  - Intention to permanently deprive:
    - Arguably unnecessary; a temporary deprivation would work better.
    - Anachronistic that conditional intent insufficient for theft but sufficient for s9(1)(a) burglary.

Check your understanding

1. Give a simple definition of theft.
2. What two important principles come from *Gomez (1993)*?
3. Explain the difference between s5(3) and s5(4).
4. How does the *Ghosh* test define dishonesty? When is the test used and why is it so important?
5. Explain two problems associated with s6.

Now test yourself

Tested ☐

1. Fill in the details in the table below to test your knowledge.

Act	Theft or no theft?	Relevant Theft Act section
Ann is in a shop and picks up a lipstick. She slips it into her pocket, thinking she will pay if she is challenged. Ann leaves the shop without paying for the lipstick.		
Brendan has had a row with his girlfriend. He sees some daffodils growing in a nearby park and picks them to give to his girlfriend as a peace offering.		
Callum goes to a restaurant with some friends. He leaves his coat behind. Next week he goes to the same restaurant and as it is raining he takes a coat from the restaurant. Unknown to Callum he has taken his own coat.		
Derek is in the supermarket. He pays with a £10 note but is given change for a £20 note. Derek realises he has too much money the next morning and the supermarket is six miles away.		
Ellen works in a busy company office. She is short of money and takes company paper and pens home for her children to use at school.		
Frank is a student who needs to photocopy a large document for an assignment. He borrows his flatmate's photocopy card, thinking his flatmate will not mind, to photocopy the document and then puts it back, although the card is out of credit when his flatmate tries to use it.		

2. Copy the table below and fill in the details to test your knowledge.

Case name	Factual key words	Area of theft	Legal importance
Lavender (1994)			
Morris (1983)			
Webster (1996)			
Easom (1971)			
Hall (1972)			
AG Ref (No 1 of 1983) (1985)			
Ghosh (1982)			
Lawrence (1972)			
DPP v Gohill (2007)			
Pitham v Hehl (1977)			
Lloyd (1985)			
Turner (No 2) (1971)			
Gomez (1993)			

(Continued)

(Continued)

Case name	Factual key words	Area of theft	Legal importance
Small (1998)			
Atakpu and Abrahams (1994)			
Ricketts (2010)			
Klineberg and Marsden (1999)			
Kelly and Lindsay (1998)			
Velumyl (1989)			
Gilks (1972)			
Oxford v Moss (1979)			
Holden (1991)			
Hinks (2000)			
Woodman (1974)			
Davidge v Bunnett (1984)			

3. Make a revision chart for theft – place cases with their relevant statutory section and make sure that definitions are clear and accurate.

Exam summary

✔ Theft is the biggest topic but be equally confident with robbery and burglary as some questions go beyond the confines of s1.

✔ **Section A** – make sure your statutory knowledge is accurate and supported by relevant cases. Be ready to make developed AO2 but read the question carefully as an essay is likely to focus on a particular aspect of this large topic.

✔ **Section B** – a question may focus solely on theft or include other Theft Act offences. Watch out for small areas in theft which you might miss without close reading. Make a plan to organise your application and only define and explain the law once

✔ **Section C** – apply principles logically and deductively and deal with both *actus reus* and *mens rea* before reaching a conclusion on each individual statement.

Striving for an A/A*?

1. Statutory knowledge needs to be sound and confident.
2. Take your research further to make your answer stand out – see **http://www.bailii.org**.
3. **Section A** – work on your analysis beforehand but be flexible to fit the question asked.
4. **Section B** – planning is essential. Practise clear and concise definitions so you can focus on accurate application.
5. **Section C** – be disciplined, logical and precise.

12 Robbery and burglary

- This chapter relates to section 8 and section 9 of the Theft Act 1968.

Robbery
Revised

Definition

- s8 – a person is guilty of robbery if he steals, and immediately before or at the time of doing so, and in order to do so, he uses force on any person or puts or seeks to put any person in fear of being then and there subjected to force.

Completed theft

- All elements of theft must be complete.
- As soon as theft is complete there can be a robbery.

Force or threat of force

- Amount of force need not be large.
- Threatening words are sufficient.
- Offence is committed even if the victim is not scared.

Force can be used on any person

- Person threatened need not be the one from whom property is taken.

When must the force be used and what must it be used for?

- Immediately before or at the time of stealing – this is interpreted generously.
- If not used in order to steal there is no robbery.

Mens rea

- Dishonesty.
- Intention to permanently deprive.
- Intention to use force to steal.

Key cases on robbery

Case name	Summary facts	Area of robbery	Legal point
Robinson (1977)	R owed £7 and during struggle R took dropped £5 note he believed man's wife owed	Need for theft	R's robbery conviction quashed as no theft based on s2(1)(a)
Corcoran v Anderton (1980)	A grabbed woman's bag which fell to ground. A ran off without bag	Need for theft	A convicted of robbery as theft complete
Dawson and James (1976)	One man pushed victim off balance so other could take wallet	Need for force or threat of force	CA upheld robbery convictions. Force ordinary word to be decided by jury
Clouden (1987)	C wrenched bag from victim's hand	Need for force or threat of force	CA upheld robbery conviction even though force quite small
B and R v DPP (2007)	Schoolboy pushed and held by other boys who took mobile phone, £5, watch and travel card. Victim shocked, not scared	Need for force or threat of force	Divisional Court QBD upheld robbery convictions as force implied by group of boys and some force used
Hale (1979)	H and accomplice broke into house. One stopped woman screaming and tied her up, while other stole property upstairs	When force used	CA upheld robbery convictions because theft as a whole was seen as a continuing event so force used at time of stealing and in order to steal
Lockley (1995)	L caught having taken beer in off-licence. Used force on shopkeeper to escape	When force used	CA upheld robbery convictions because theft as a whole was seen as a continuing event so force used at time of stealing and in order to steal

Burglary

Revised

Definition

- s9(1)(a) – entry of a building or part of a building as a trespasser with intent to steal, inflict GBH or do unlawful damage to the building or anything in it.
- s9(1)(b) – having entered a building or part of a building as a trespasser a person steals or attempts to steal anything in the building or inflicts or attempts to inflict GBH on any person in the building.

Common elements

Revised

Entry

- Developed by the judges.
- Actual entry is not required.

A building or part of a building

- No definition in the Theft Act.
- Judicial decisions have included houseboats and caravans.
- Less permanent structures have been problematic.
- Part of a building – access is open only to some parts of the building.

A trespasser

- Someone who enters without permission.
- Defendant must know that they are trespassing or be subjectively reckless as to whether they are trespassing.
- Possible to become a trespasser by exceeding permission given.

Example

In the Australian case of *Barker v R (1983)* B was asked to keep an eye on his neighbour's house and told where there was a key in case of an emergency. B used the key to enter his neighbour's house and steal; he was convicted of burglary.

Mens rea

- For both s9(1)(a) and (b) the defendant must know or be subjectively reckless as to whether he is trespassing.
- For s9(1)(a) the defendant must intend to commit one of the three ulterior offences and conditional intent is sufficient.
- For s9(1)(b) the defendant must also have the *mens rea* for theft or GBH when committing or attempting to commit the *actus reus* of one of these offences.

Key cases on burglary

Case name	Summary facts	Element of burglary	Legal point
Collins (1972)	C climbed ladder naked except for socks and perched on windowsill before entering and having sex with girl	Entry	CA quashed C's burglary conviction saying entry had to be 'effective and substantial'
Brown (1985)	B leaned through shop window to reach goods inside	Entry	CA upheld B's conviction for burglary saying entry had to be 'effective'
Ryan (1996)	R got stuck trying to break into house in middle of night with head and one arm inside building	Entry	CA upheld R's burglary conviction although entry ineffective
B and S v Leathley (1979)	25-foot-long freezer container resting on sleepers in farmyard for two years with lockable doors and electricity	Building	Held to be a building
Norfolk Constabulary v Seekings and Gould (1986)	Lorry trailer with wheels used for storage for over a year with access steps and electricity	Building	Not a building as still had wheels
Walkington (1979)	W opened till inside area of shop surrounded by three-sided counter	Part of a building	W's s9(1)(a) conviction upheld; inside counter part of building where W was trespasser who entered intending to steal
Jones and Smith (1976)	S and J took two TV sets from home of S's father, who said son had general right to enter	Trespass	CA upheld burglary convictions as permission given was exceeded

Points for an essay

- Inconsistency as in theft appropriation occurs at one moment in time but in robbery theft can be a continuing event.
- Inconsistency between robbery and burglary as in robbery a theft is necessary whereas in burglary conviction can be based on an intention to steal or an attempted theft.
- Level of force required in robbery is low; this is sometimes problematic for a jury.
- Arguable whether the Theft Act gives effect to Parliament's intentions, as the Criminal Law Revision Committee report did not anticipate such force as snatching a bag from someone who does not fight back being robbery.
- Robbery and burglary maximum sentences can seem high but justified due to fear caused and invasion of homes where people should feel safe.
- Burglary can be confusing as in s9(1)(a) there must be an intention at the time of entry whereas for s9(1)(b) the only *mens rea* which needs to be proved is that for the offence attempted or committed once the defendant has entered as a trespasser.
- Many burglary key terms are not defined, particularly 'entry' and what constitutes a building.
- The word 'trespasser' is unhelpful as it is also in civil law; its meaning in criminal law goes further as there is a need for *mens rea* with regard to trespass.
- Arguably it is peculiar to extend liability to those who exceed permission to be in a building or part of a building. Justification may be higher sentencing but for most people caught by this extension theft would be adequate.
- Arguable whether burglary is fit for purpose given the number of offences committed.

Check your understanding

1. Give a simple definition of robbery.
2. What is the potential problem with the decision in *Corcoran v Anderton (1980)*?
3. Give a simple definition of s9(1)(a).
4. How does the definition for s9(1)(b) differ?
5. What is the significance of the decision in *Ryan (1996)*?

Now test yourself

Tested

1. For each of the scenarios shown below decide whether an offence of robbery or burglary has been committed, giving reasons for your answer.

Act	Offence or no offence?
Mike walks up to Nathan and says, 'Give me £10'. Nathan hands over £10.	
Oliver is wearing a Rolex watch. Patrick runs up to Oliver and grabs his arm, demanding that Oliver take his watch off. Oliver refuses but drops his mobile phone and Patrick runs off with Oliver's phone.	
Quentin goes into a shop intending to get some new jeans by trying a pair on and then walking out of the shop wearing them. He tries on several pairs of jeans but none fit and he leaves the shop still wearing his old jeans.	
Richard breaks into a nearby house as he knows the owner has lots of antique silver and is on holiday. Inside the house all the silver has been locked away. Richard is so angry he finds a jar of curry sauce and throws it on the white carpet in the living room.	
Trevor is at a pop festival and sees that the girl in a nearby tent has a very expensive camera. When the girl goes to see a band Trevor reaches into the girl's tent and takes the camera.	

2. Copy the table below and fill in the details to test your knowledge.

Case name	Factual key words	Area of law	Legal importance
Ryan (1996)			
Robinson (1977)			
Barker (1983)			
Lockley (1995)			
Corcoran v Anderton (1980)			
Walkington (1979)			
B and R v DPP (2007)			
Collins (1972)			
Jones and Smith (1976)			
B and S v Leathley (1979)			
Clouden (1987)			
Brown (1985)			
Dawson and James (1976)			
Hale (1979)			

3. Make a revision mind map with cases grouped under a clear statutory definition for each offence.

Exam summary

✔ **Section A** – make sure you have some AO2 points ready. There is some overlap with theft and development helps you reach the higher mark bands.

✔ **Section B** – robbery and burglary are likely to appear alongside other offences and so you must be able to identify, define, explain and apply the law clearly.

✔ **Section C** – you need to apply the principles behind robbery and burglary logically. Consider *actus reus* first and then move on to the *mens rea* before reaching a conclusion based on the statement.

Striving for an A/A*?

1. Be confident in your statutory definitions.
2. Take your research further, for example, read about crime figures for these and other offences at **http://www.homeoffice.gov.uk/science-research/research-statistics/crime/crime-statistics**.
3. **Section A** – think beyond the most obvious points; linking to wider issues in theft and the policy implications of such important offences will give your essay depth.
4. **Section B** – demonstrate clear, thorough and confident application skills. Pay particular attention to burglary definitions – they often catch candidates out!
5. **Section C** – read the statement carefully and do exactly as it asks.

G154 Special Study Paper

About this section

This part of the revision guide has been written to cover the OCR A2 G154 Criminal Law Special Study module. The G154 module is synoptic and, as such, requires you to demonstrate your understanding of the connections and links between the main theme covered and other relevant areas of OCR's A Level Law specification. This therefore includes the G153 Criminal Law module and also the OCR AS Level specification's English Legal System (G151) and Sources of Law (G152) modules.

There are four sections to this part of the revision guide. As you will be aware, the G154 theme changes each year. As such, this part of the guide covers the skills required to tackle the G154 exam paper. For specific revision notes on the yearly themes, please refer to the contents pages of this book.

Part 1 is the Introduction which provides general guidance on the G154 paper.

Part 2 covers 'How to use the pre-release source materials' to enable you to begin your exploration of the G154 theme.

Part 3 covers 'Decoding the Special Study paper'. This will provide you with specific guidance on the demands of each question required to tackle the G154 paper.

Part 4 looks at exemplar student responses for a potential higher-, mid- or lower-level answer. All three G154 questions are looked at and an exam comment is provided for each answer.

1 Introduction

The synoptic element

There are three major areas for students to concentrate on in the Special Study, regardless of the year they sit the exam. The first is knowledge of the G154 theme. This theme changes each year. Second, and equally as crucial, is the student's understanding of the specific skills that are required to answer the questions. The final area is the student's awareness of and ability to utilise fully the OCR Criminal Law pre-release materials.

The paper for G154 is synoptic, in other words it is an outline or summary of the theme. You are required to demonstrate your synoptic thinking through your understanding of this theme via a case discussion, an essay and in a series of problem scenarios. When approaching the case discussion and the essay, you must position the overall theme in the context of:

- the role judges have played in developing, or not, the law
- the use of judicial precedent
- the role of Parliament in providing statutory materials
- the role of law reform agencies who have made, where relevant, proposals to the development of the law.

Some assistance is given through the pre-release materials:

> **Exam tip**
>
> Success in the G154 exam is not due solely to your knowledge of the topic area; it is also about what you do with that knowledge in order to answer the questions.

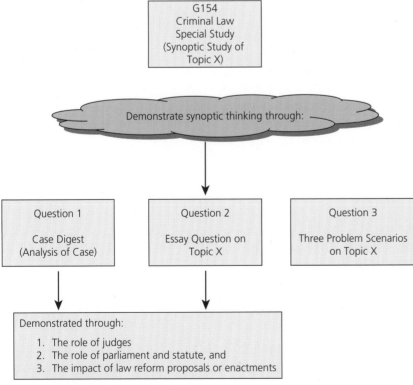

Figure 1 Demonstrating synoptic thinking

For both the G153 Criminal Law and the G154 Criminal Law Special Study, the response to a question in the exam is marked into one of three assessment objectives groupings: AO1, AO2 and AO3, dependent upon the demands of the question. You are therefore expected to demonstrate the following:

- **AO1** – Knowledge and understanding of legal rules and principles by selecting and explaining relevant information and illustrating with examples and citation. For G154 this would include definitions of the law from statute or the common law, relevant case names, facts and judgments.

- **AO2** – Analyse legal material, issues and situations, and evaluate and apply the appropriate legal rules and principles. For G154 this would require the student to provide comment on the law and how it has been applied to the benefit or detriment of those involved. In certain situations it also requires the application of legal rules in scenario-based situations.

- **AO3** – Present a logical and coherent argument and communicate relevant material in a clear and effective manner using appropriate legal terminology. This is an automatic mark dependent on the AO1 and/or AO2 demands of the question. The higher the mark for AO1 and/or AO2, the higher the AO3 mark. This is due to the quality of your response to the question.

It is also important that you are aware of the OCR A2 Law Levels of assessment. In order to score marks, AO1 and AO2 are divided up into five Levels, Level 5 scoring the highest marks. AO3 is divided up into four Levels. In order to achieve a Level 5 response for AO1, your response must contain material that is wide-ranging, accurate and showing detailed knowledge with a clear and confident understanding of the relevant concepts and principles. Where appropriate, you must be able to elaborate with wide citation of relevant statutes and case law.

In order to achieve a Level 5 response for AO2 you must show an ability to identify correctly the relevant and important points of criticism of the law. This must show good understanding of any current debate and any proposals for reform, or identify all of the relevant points of law in issue. You must also show a high level of ability to develop arguments or apply points of law accurately and pertinently to a given factual situation, and reach a cogent, logical and well informed conclusion.

As discussed below, it is crucial to maximise the AO2 mark since this assessment objective carries most of the marks for the G154 paper. The crucial issue with AO2 therefore is your ability to critically analyse the G154 theme. Some suggestions would be:

- Deconstruct each of the Sources 1–6 from the pre-release materials. In particular, look for the author's own comments and analysis.

- Develop an ability to comment on all the AO1 factual information. In particular:

- Look at the statute: does it make sense? Does it do what it was meant to do? If not, why not?

- Look at the case judgements: are they sensible? Do they benefit the public or subsequent defendants who face a similar charge? Producing a critical analysis of the G154 theme is your opportunity to explore the existing (and sometimes well trodden) academic analysis, as well as sharing your own opinions. The latter is greatly encouraged for the G154 paper, but remember that you must be able to back them up.

- Use the availability of law reform agencies' recommendations. Many areas of law have had such recommendations made by, for example, the Law Commission, and many current laws were as a result of recommendations made by such agencies.

The AO2 mark

How to maximise the AO2 mark

- For responses to questions 1 and 2, one of the most straightforward ways to analyse or evaluate the question set is to try and comment on all the factual information you introduce as AO1. In many cases the comment will be that traditionally used in textbooks or in discussion in class. However, there is also opportunity for you to introduce your own ideas, some of which may have never been considered by others before. If it is relevant then it is worthy of credit by the examiner. Look at previous mark schemes where you will find that you can be credited for any relevant comment where justified.

- Question 1 is a case digest, requiring you to discuss the impact or lack of impact, of a particular case. This analysis, albeit on a smaller scale, can be used for responses to Question 2. Here, one of the most obvious ways to comment is during or after AO1 discussion of cases. Simply because a case was decided in a particular way, e.g. in the Court of Appeal, does not mean you have to agree, and in many cases you should not necessarily agree, particularly when applying an older case in a changing modern context.

- Pre-exam preparation for AO2 is also beneficial. While the source material contains some crucial AO2 points, creating a list of specific or general AO2 points is just as important, if not more important than memorising definitions and case names and facts. It is important to develop arguments rather than simply assemble points.

- You are advised to extend your arguments to their natural conclusion even if this is contrary to the law – this furthers your own analysis.

- On a very basic level you can make analytical links between groups of facts you have learnt for your AO1.

- As stated above you can employ the same analytical mechanisms for the G154 paper as you have previously adopted in your AS year. While studying the topic, you should be looking back and commenting on areas like precedent, the interpretation of statute law and commenting on the role of the judge in the development of law and on justice and morality.

- Refer to any Law Commission or similar recommendations on the reform of the law on the topic under consideration.

Exam tip

It is very important for students to be aware that nearly 60 per cent of the total marks on the G154 exam paper are awarded for AO2. Therefore, depending upon which question is being answered, analysis, evaluation or application carries the highest of all marks in total for the paper.

That is not to say that AO1 is not important, but the AO2 mark is higher to make students aware that it is one thing to be able to recite the law but it is even more appropriate to be able to understand how this works in practice and be able to comment upon it or apply it.

- For Question 3, the AO2 mark is in the application of the AO1 to the problem scenario. There are no marks for the evaluation of the law for this question. Various techniques have been developed by Law teachers, for example, using the memory aids such as ILAC (Issues, Law, Application and Conclusion) or IDEA (Identify, Describe, Evaluate and Apply/Analyse).

Exam tip

Create a list of specific or general AO2 points via a timeline for the topic to provide a framework for your response.

The three key skills

Revised

As with all exams, you must adopt a strategy in order to justify yourself. Simply knowing the law word perfect is not enough. This may be beneficial to the AO1 mark but the G154 paper requires you to synthesise your responses and not to simply tell the examiner everything you know about the topic. When tackling the G154 paper, you need to demonstrate three key skills:

Assessment objective weightings

Remember the weightings for each of the three assessment objectives. The total paper, which is marked out of 80, is divided up into assessment objectives and marked accordingly. The percentage marks are as follows:

- **AO1** – 32.5%
- **AO2** – 57.5%
- **AO3** – 10%

Time management

You must have effective time management: while practising writing out specimen answers is a skill learned before the exam, and one that is encouraged, you MUST stick to a time frame or you risk spending too much time on a specific question to the detriment of the others. The approximate times (ignoring AO3 in Questions 1 and 2 since it is an automatically allocated mark) for answering the Special Study questions are:

- **Question 1** – 15 minutes for 12 marks.
- **Question 2** – 37.5 minutes for 30 marks
- **Question 3** – 37.5 minutes for 30 marks

Effective reading skills

There are two crucial factors here:

1. The first factor is your pre-exam preparation, which involves more than reading the source materials. Remember that the breadth of materials you use is important: to simply look at one or two textbooks ignores other widely available analysis of the topic. Newspapers and other news media, together with legal magazines (especially those aimed at A Level learners) are of particular importance.

2. The second factor is in the reading done during the exam itself. Many a well prepared student has damaged their chances of success by not reading the question on the exam paper and has instead answered the question they hoped to see. The G154 exam does not require you to tell the examiner everything you know about topic X. It is an exercise in synthesising the topic to explore its successes and its failures in the English legal system.

Typical mistake

Many students do not read the question on the exam paper and instead answer the question they wanted or expected to see.

2 How to use the pre-release source material

One of the key advantages of the G154 exam is that pre-release source materials are available to students which cover the main parts of the topic area. The source materials are available well in advance of the exam and the purpose of the materials is to provide key narrative and comment on the topic. This is to provide a starting point for students to analyse the materials before deciding how they wish to pursue their research on the topic. There are six sources. These are based around academic writing in the form of part of a legal textbook or journal and excerpts from judges' actual case decisions relevant to the topic. A new copy is provided in the exam for students' use.

Using the source material   Revised ☐

Quote if appropriate

- It is perfectly acceptable to use the sources by quoting small amounts of what is said in them.
- Rather than having to write, for example, the whole section of an Act of Parliament in your exam, you can simply quote (accurately) the relevant source and line numbers, thus saving time.

Remember the importance of development

- When carrying out your research you should not treat each source in isolation.
- Look back to the previous source and forward to the next source to see how, if relevant, the law has been developed.

Identify the useful information and comment

- Deconstructing each of the sources is an important process that you must go through before you move on to further research.

Look for the AO1 and AO2 in each source

- In extracts from textbooks, in among the narrative of the law, the author(s) will pass comment. This should be separated out and form a start to or part of your own evaluation of the law.
- The same also applies to the judges and their decisions.

Going beyond the source materials

- The sources do not provide all of the law.
- While each of the sources provides information and analysis, there is an expectation that you will not simply concentrate all of your research on the sources themselves.

> **Exam tip**
>
> You can achieve higher marks by looking outside the source materials to further your answers. For example, a missed opportunity would be to ignore any government or Law Commission report on the topic area for an answer to Question 1 or 2.

3 Decoding the Special Study paper

Having looked at the general skills required for the G154 paper, this section looks at the more specific skills that you need to be aware of and work toward for each question. The G154 paper tests you by using three separate questions. Each question looks at different approaches to the topic area. As a result, each question examines different skills that you need to be aware of. Each question is looked at below and advice is given on the skills required, together with details of some of the common problems that are repeated by students when answering such questions.

The demands of Question 1 — Revised ☐

Question 1 is referred to as being a digest of one of the eight cases mentioned in the pre-release source material. This means the examiner is looking for the student's evaluation on how important, or not, the case was in developing the law.

The specific demands of Question 1 are shown below.

Answer the question set by the examiner

If the question is about case X, then you must use case X as the thrust of your answer and how important, or not, in your opinion it has been to the development of the law. It is important to state somewhere in your answer *why* case X is important in developing the law, or not. This may be in the introduction, conclusion or throughout your answer.

Timing

- As discussed above, you must spend no more than 15 minutes on this question, as failure to do so will impact on the other two questions which are worth more marks.

- Thorough preparation will prevent you using valuable time which should be allocated to the other questions.

Use of the pre-release special study materials

- Once you have drawn a timeline for each case, you should then look at the pre-release material and note down everything you can about the case.

- Many important pieces of information are contained in the pre-release materials to assist you in forming your own opinion of the case and its impact on the law.

Only AO2 marks are scored

- Although an automatic mark is given for AO3, this is awarded depending on how good your AO2 mark is. Therefore, you must evaluate the case's impact on the law.

> **Exam tip**
>
> When researching each case use a timeline. Placing the question's case on a timeline allows you to note the significant cases and/or statutory interventions that have occurred before and after the case. It also helps you to see which cases came before or after that case: perhaps Question 1's case was as a result of a clarification point from a previous LC (Linked Case), or perhaps the LC tried to clarify what the Question 1's case had stated as its *ratio*, etc.

> **Typical mistake**
>
> Many students fail to score highly on Question 1 because they answer it, essentially, on another case. This may be due to the fact they have taken the risky strategy of question spotting and failed to research case X, answering on case Y instead.

● There is no AO1 mark so if you simply describe the law you will not be rewarded for doing this.

The Critical Point

Three marks are available where the student discusses what is known as the critical point (CP). How well you discuss the CP will dictate your mark. A rough rule of thumb for three marks would be: the CP is stated, then developed, then well developed. The CP is, in effect, the *ratio decidendi* of the case in question. This should be easy for you to find in textbooks.

The Analytical Points

A maximum of six marks is awarded to students who further explain why the case has developed the law, separate from the CP. Previous OCR G154 mark schemes provide further examples and the exemplar material below reflects this. The mark scheme is not prescriptive, that is to say, you do not have to analyse the case in exactly the same way as the examiner has; rather, you are credited for the most common points of analysis that have been raised in textbooks for example, or in class. This also gives you the opportunity to comment in ways that, if relevant, have not been seen before.

The Linked Case

The final three marks are awarded where the student discusses a linked case (LC). Clearly the LC must be a linked to the case featured in Question 1 and it must be placed in the context as to how it is a LC.

> **Typical mistake**
>
> Students often fail to gain high marks where they discuss, at great length, many linked cases when only one case would be sufficient. However, the one case discussed must be well developed and contextualised in light of the main case.

The demands of Question 2

Revised ☐

This is an essay-based question which looks at the whole or part of the topic in greater detail and is similar in many ways to a Part A question on the G153 Criminal Law exam paper. The AO1 mark is based upon your description of the relevant law, while the AO2 mark is based on both your response to the question's quote and other relevant evaluation and analysis on the topic area.

The specific demands of Question 2 are as follows:

Answer the question set by the examiner

Again, as discussed above for Question 1, you must answer the question set, not the one you would prefer. While this may seem like common sense, students can ignore the specific command of the question which, for example, requires a discussion on a specific part of the topic rather than on the whole topic itself, or vice versa.

Timing

You should spend no longer than 37.5 minutes on this question. If you do spend longer, this will impact on the time available to spend on another question. A tip here would be to practise writing out a potential response to a Question 2 and time yourself doing this.

AO1

A maximum of 16 marks is available for AO1. It is good practice to prepare the AO1 for the topic area. However, you must be able to discuss the whole topic or part of it, depending upon the specific question set.

AO2

A maximum of 14 marks is available for AO2. This is essentially awarded for two areas. The first is where you evaluate the topic in the context of the question's quote. The second is where you evaluate the topic in a more general style. This will be either from well established analysis, possibly in class and/or from textbooks, etc., or is simply your own valid opinion on the topic.

Use of the pre-release source materials

Clearly, textbooks and reputable internet sites are a good source of both AO1 and AO2. However, well prepared students will first look at the source material before moving on to their further research. See Part 2 above for how best to use the pre-release source material.

Line references

Since time is clearly a factor in answering Question 2, you can refer to line references in the source if you are simply rewriting relevant parts of the source. This is particularly true where definitions of the law or case facts are used in the source. Rather than write something that the source states, you can instead use the format: *as stated in Source X, lines Y-Z*. Any source reference must be discrete. That is to say, you must not simply say the law is in Source X and leave it at that!

Cases

For each Level of Assessment (1–5) for AO1, the G154 paper requires that you must name a specific number of relevant cases and within that number of cases a certain number must be well developed. Specifically:

- **For Level 5** – there must be a minimum of eight relevant, linked cases, with a minimum of six cases well developed.
- **For Level 3** – there must be a minimum of four relevant, linked cases, with a minimum of two cases well developed.
- **For Level 1** – there is no expectation that the student will use any cases.

A well developed case is defined as being one which does more than simply name a relevant case. This could include an accurate description of the facts, *ratio decidendi* or other relevant explanation of the case.

> **Typical mistake**
>
> Failure to refer to or mention the quote will prevent you achieving top marks as you simply aren't answering the question.

> **Exam tip**
>
> Where the topic has common law clarification in the form of cases, a useful tip for students is to comment on how a case they have mentioned has impacted on the topic. This can be in the same vein as a Question 1 case but in a much lesser way.

The demands of Question 3 — Revised

Question 3 requires you to focus on three problem or scenario-type situations based on the topic area. You must describe (for AO1) and more importantly apply (for AO2) the law to each situation given.

When answering Question 3 you can use the skills you have acquired in answering a Part B question on the G153 Criminal Law exam paper.

However, where the G153 Part B problem question has perhaps four or five issues that you must identify and discuss, the G154 Question 3 centres on one issue based on the topic area.

The specific demands of Question 3 are as follows.

Timing

As with Question 2, you should spend no longer than 37.5 minutes on this question. If you exceed this time you will impact on the time available to spend on another question.

Structured answer

In order to answer the question you must define (or refer to the law using an accurate reference to the source materials) for the AO1 mark. Once this is done, each part of the relevant definition of the law must be applied to the scenario specifically in order to achieve the AO2 marks for application.

Note the assessment objective weightings

For each part of Question 3 (a), (b) and (c) roughly 3 marks maximum are allocated for AO1 description, 6 marks maximum for AO2 application and a final mark for an accurate conclusion.

Scenarios similar to actual cases

Many Question 3 scenarios have their origins in actual pre-decided cases. You are therefore advised to follow such a thought process when answering the question and note in particular if the scenario has a twist not reflected in the pre-decided case.

The conclusion

Having defined and applied the law to the scenario, you must conclude your response for each scenario – this is worth one mark if accurate. You cannot get full marks for each part of Question 3 unless you do so. You must therefore answer Question 3's stem question by accurately stating whether the defendant is guilty or not guilty of an offence. Responses using words like possibly guilty/not guilty or might be guilty/not guilty are not creditworthy since they do not provide a definitive conclusion.

> **Typical mistake**
>
> Two common faults made by students in their responses to Question 3 scenarios are where they evaluate the law or where they provide a suggestion of sentencing possibilities. For example, 'the defendant should get six months.' Neither is relevant or creditworthy.

4 Exemplar student responses for G154

This part of the book provides examples of responses to the three types of questions set for the G154 exam. Each question is looked at with three types of responses: a higher-level response, a mid-level response and a lower-level response. Following each response there is an examiner comment on how this particular answer reached the level it did.

Before looking at the exemplar responses it is important to note the OCR level descriptors that are available either in mark schemes or on the OCR A Level Law specification. As they mark your exam paper, examiners will award a mark for AO1 or AO2 (depending upon the question) based around a level descriptor. You are advised to familiarise yourself with the level descriptors.

Higher-level response   Revised ☐

In a higher-level response students:

For AO1 – an ability to provide a response that:

- is wide-ranging across the topic area for Questions 2 and 3. This does not have to cover every part in minute detail but enough to produce such a response
- is accurate in their narrative of definitions, cases and any other AO1 discussion
- has a detailed knowledge of the topic area relevant to Questions 2 and 3
- has a clear and confident understanding of relevant concepts and principles for the topic area and includes few, if any, mistakes in their responses
- where appropriate, demonstrates their ability to go beyond simply the basics of the topic by being able to use a wide citation of relevant statutes and case law.

For AO2 – an ability to provide a response that:

- is able to correctly identify relevant and important points of criticism of the topic area
- shows a good understanding of current debate and proposals for reform where relevant, or identifies all of the relevant points of law in issue
- has a high level of ability to develop arguments, or is able to apply points of law accurately and pertinently to a given factual situation and reach a cogent, logical and well informed conclusion.

Mid-level response

In a mid-level response students are demonstrating:

For AO1 – an ability to provide a response that:

- has adequate knowledge of the topic
- shows reasonable understanding of the relevant concepts and principles of the topic
- where appropriate, shows ability to elaborate with some citation of relevant statutes and case law for the topic.

For AO2 – an ability to provide a response that:

- shows an ability to analyse most of the more obvious points central to the question
- is able to identify the main points of law in issue for the topic
- shows an ability to develop arguments or apply points of law mechanically to a given factual situation and reach a conclusion for the question.

Lower-level response

In a lower-level response students are demonstrating:

For AO1 – an ability to provide a response that:

- has limited or very limited knowledge of the basic concepts and principles
- provides limited points of detail
- has no expectation by the examiner for accurate citation of relevant statutes and case law.

For AO2 – an ability to provide a response that:

- is able to explain at least one of the simpler points central to the question
- has identified at least one of the points of law in issue for the question
- takes an approach which may be uncritical and/or unselective in relation to the question set.

G154 Question 1

Discuss the importance of the decision in Jones (Special Study Material Source 3, page 4) to the development of the law on attempted crimes. (16 marks)

Higher-level response

The facts for *Jones* can be found in Source 3, lines 1–7. This question is about the definition in the law on attempts defined in section 1 of the Criminal Attempts Act 1981 (Source 1, lines 10–13). Ultimately the defendant was convicted of attempted murder. This case was decided on whether the defendant had done an act that was more than merely preparatory to the commission of the offence.

The initial acts in the case were seen to be merely preparatory, such as buying the gun and shortening the barrel (Source 3, lines 11–13). However, once the defendant had entered the car and pointed the gun his acts were said to be 'more than merely preparatory'. Even though he had not yet completed the last act of removing the safety trigger, it was enough to be an attempt.

There are a number of common law tests that could link to *Jones*. The last act/proximity test put forward by *Eagleton* would link as *Jones* had not yet done this, therefore he may have been found not guilty under the old common law test. Lord Diplock's 'Rubicon' test could also be applied to *Jones* as he could have been seen to have 'passed the point of no return'. These tests have now been abolished by the Criminal Attempts Act 1981 and are no longer valid.

A case linked with *Jones* is *Gullefer* as he had also not performed the last act. The case had defined the *actus reus* of attempts as being where D had embarked upon the crime proper. In *Gullefer*, the court felt that since D had many acts yet to accomplish before committing the full crime, D was only at the mere preparation stage. This case was later referred to in *Jones* by the Court of Appeal.

The question put to the judge was whether there was enough evidence from which a reasonable jury could find that the defendant had passed the stage of more than merely preparatory. Clearly, this was possible in *Jones* and the Court of Appeal in *Jones* felt that whether he had or had not was a matter for the jury to decide, having looked at the plain ordinary meaning of the words of section 1 (Source 3, lines 8–11). The critical part of *Jones* is that Taylor LJ said this and to not refer back to the old common law tests and in doing so cleared the confusion on what is more than merely preparatory.

Jones's importance to the development to the law was that it clarified how far a defendant had to go to reach a more than merely preparatory stage. Cases of *Gullefer*, *Geddes* and *Campbell* required further acts to be convicted. In *Jones* the defendant had carried out further acts.

Reforms were put forward by the Law Commission in 2007 where two new offences are suggested to replace section 1. It would be said that *Jones* would still be guilty under this reform but *Geddes* and *Campbell* would now be convicted under criminal preparation at least.

Exam comment

This is an excellent response. The student has a clear understanding of the case and is able to analyse and comment on its importance to the development of the law. They begin by contextualising their answer within the topic area and even before they provide their analysis, have summarised what the case stands for and have used source references to do so.

In the remaining paragraphs the student provides more detailed analysis of the case:

Paragraph 2: here the student provides comment on where the Court of Appeal had explained, in their opinion, where exactly the *actus reus* of the law on attempt could be found and which acts would fall short in *Jones'* situation.

Paragraph 3: this analyses the now defunct common law tests and indeed applies them to *Jones*. The student then explains that the tests were decided as being no longer relevant.

Paragraph 4: the case of *Gullefer* is linked to *Jones*. The student explains part of the decision in *Gullefer* and how the court decided his fate based on this. They then state why *Gullefer* is linked to *Jones*.

Paragraph 5: the critical point of *Jones* is discussed here. However, rather than write out the exact quotes, the student uses the source material for assistance to provide more time for analysis.

Paragraph 6: here the student provides a short summary on how the case was important to the development of the law.

Paragraph 7: this provides a final point of analysis by commenting on what the Law Commission had said about reforming the law and interestingly looks at the impact of this on *Jones*.

Mid-level response

Section 1(1) of the Criminal Attempts Act 1981 states that 'if a person does an act which is more than merely preparatory to the commission of the offence, he is guilty of attempting to commit the offence'.

In *Jones* (Source 3, lines 1–17) the defendant's girlfriend no longer wanted to continue their relationship and moved on to another man who was the victim. One day he took himself to the victim's daughter's school and got into his car with a loaded shotgun. He pointed it at him and said, 'You're not going to like this'. The victim wrestled with him and managed to grab the gun from the defendant and ran off.

The old common law tests were ignored by Taylor LJ in *Jones*.

Following the previous case of *Gullefer*, where Lord Lane introduced the idea of looking at the plain and natural meaning of the words in section 1 and whether the defendant was 'embarking on the crime proper', it was decided that there was sufficient evidence in *Jones* to be left to the jury, which consequently convicted the defendant as a result of attempted murder. After *Jones*, *Geddes* introduced the rule of 'moving from planning to preparation to execution and implementation'. This was a significant case to the development of the law.

Exam comment

The candidate begins their response by simply stating AO1 points. In other words, they both define the definition and state the facts of the case. Since the definition of the law is AO1 and the facts of the case without commenting on them is AO1, no credit is gained here, therefore wasting time.

Nevertheless, the candidate then begins to make some analytical comment about the old common law tests, but doesn't provide any further explanation of these comments other than that they were 'ignored'.

The final paragraph provides a very brief run through of a linked case (*Gullefer*), the critical point ('left to the jury') then back to a linked case (*Geddes*).

This response is all too brief. Had the candidate explained or dwelled on the important issues raised, this further explanation would have resulted in more AO2 marks. In effect, their response is a very brief summary of what is important about the case, analysing the obvious points but doing very little with them.

Student activity

Identify three things that this candidate could have done to improve their response for both AO1 and AO2.

Lower-level response

Jones is a case stated under the *actus reus* of attempts and discusses how section 1 of the Criminal Attempts Act defines this as being 'if a person does an act which is more than merely preparatory to the commission of the offence, he is guilty of attempting to commit the offence'.

The defendant had got into a car belonging to the new boyfriend and had pulled out a gun from his bag and was found guilty of attempted murder.

This case developed the law since it decided what was more than merely preparatory and how far a person must go before they can be said to be more than merely preparatory.

The victim must be in danger and fear for his life. It is clear in this case he had the necessary *mens rea* for the crime since he had intended to kill the victim, even though in court he said that he didn't. In other cases the intent may not be so clear so the act must be dangerous before it will be an attempt.

Exam comment

The candidate clearly understands the context the case is part of. The candidate spends part of their answer stating what is AO1 description – the definition of the law and the facts of the case without commenting or applying the facts to the law. They are aware that the case developed the law by stating some analysis as to what the case was, in essence, about. However, they end their answer by discussing a point unrelated to the question.

Student activity

Identify five things that this candidate could have done to improve their response for both AO1 and AO2.

G154 Question 2

Revised

In Source 2 (Special Study Material page 3, lines 16–17) Bingham LJ asks: 'Had [the defendant] moved from the realm of ... preparation and planning into the area of execution or implementation?'

Discuss how accurately the above statement reflects the ways in which the law on the actus reus of attempted crimes has developed. (34 marks)

Higher-level response

The law on attempts is governed by the Criminal Attempts Act 1981. Previous to the Act the law was governed by the common law which devised a number of tests to decide whether the defendant (D) was guilty of an attempt or not.

For example, the proximity test which was created in *Eagleton* which looked backwards from the main offence to see if they were immediately connected to the *actus reus*. This was applied in *Robinson* where D attempted to defraud an insurance company after staging a robbery. The court quashed his conviction because he had further acts to carry out, for example, making a claim to his insurers. Only acts immediately connected should be considered an attempt and not acts remotely connected.

Additionally there was the Rubicon test which was created in *Stonehouse* and used in *Widdowson*. This states that an attempt takes place when D has 'crossed the Rubicon' and 'burnt his boats' and thus passed the point of no return.

The statement is accurate in some ways as some cases' tests have helped show that D has moved from the realm of planning to execution as they have been convicted, showing that the law on attempts has been developed by the courts. However, before the Act the tests were criticised since there was more than one, and depending on which test was used by the court, it was argued, could produce different results.

The *actus reus* of attempts states that an attempt takes place where the defendant has carried out an act which is deemed more than merely preparatory. This is defined in Source 1, lines 10–13.

In the case of *Boyle and Boyle (1987)* the Ds were found outside a building where the hinge and lock had been broken. They were found guilty of attempted burglary. Unusually, since this was a case after the Act, the court found them guilty using an old common law test called the 'series of acts' test to reach their decision. Even though this secured a just conviction it shows the accuracy of the statement as the law hadn't developed after the Act as the courts were still using old common law tests.

While this case was an anomaly in using old law, most of the cases after 1981 have tried to define what is meant by more than merely preparatory. For example:

In *Gullefer* D placed a bet on a dog but during the race he realised it wasn't going to win so he jumped on the track to get the race voided. He was charged with attempted theft but his conviction was quashed. This again shows the accuracy of the statement is true. Lord Lane tried to explain what the *actus reus* meant by saying the jury must ask whether D's merely preparatory acts had ended and he had 'embarked on the crime proper' (Source 1, lines 27–31) in order for it to be an attempt. This helped the law by giving an explanation as to the *actus reus* but in doing so created another test for the jury to consider which probably wasn't meant by Parliament when enacting s1(1).

In the attempted murder case of *Jones*, D bought a shotgun, shortened the barrel and got into the victim's car. He pointed the gun at the victim and said, 'You're not going to like this!' Referring back to *Gullefer* the court stated that the plain natural meaning of the words of s1(1) must be used by the jury to decide whether it was an attempt. They felt that there was a clear dividing line between D's preparatory acts (e.g. obtaining the gun and going to the victim) and those that were more than merely preparatory (e.g. pointing the gun at the victim with the intention to kill – Source 3, lines 11–16). The D was clearly culpable and adhered to the intentions of the Law Commission of 1980.

In *Campbell* a controversial decision was made. D was arrested outside a post office while in possession of a threatening note and an imitation gun. He was charged with attempted robbery but his conviction was quashed (Source 1 lines 21–26). This was because his acts were not more than merely preparatory. This was an unjust decision as D was clearly culpable and was just yards from entering the post office. This shows the law on attempts has not developed properly as D had clearly moved from planning to implementation. However, the court felt that there were too many acts left before the jury could safely say he was more than merely preparatory. However, this leaves the police in a difficult situation if they know someone is about to carry out a crime. Would they have to wait until the very last moment in a dangerous situation before they decided to arrest someone? This could endanger life. The Law Commission in 2007 disagreed with the decision in *Campbell* and suggested a new offence of criminal preparation which would have covered this situation.

In *Geddes*, D's conviction was quashed. He had been convicted of attempted false imprisonment when he had been spotted in the boys' toilets of a school. When he ran off he left a holdall containing a knife, rope and masking tape. The court stated that he clearly had the intent to carry out the full offence, however his acts had simply not gone far enough to satisfy the *actus reus* of attempts. As shown in the statement in Source 2, lines 16–17, Lord Bingham created further clarification by stating that a jury should ask themselves if D had moved from planning and preparation into execution and implementation and was he doing an act that showed he was actually trying to commit the offence? While the decision remains controversial, the fact that there has been further clarification of the *actus reus* is a good thing.

Further cases of *Nash* and *Toothill* show the accuracy of the statement. In *Nash*, D had written two letters to his paperboy asking him to engage in sexual activities. Watched by the police he went to meet paperboy and they arrested D. He was convicted as the court held that in meeting the paperboy he had moved into the execution of his plan. In *Toothill*, D was arrested in a garden after the homeowner had seen him masturbating there. He was charged with attempted burglary (rape). Whilst both these decisions are correct, it is arguable that they still had acts to carry out: in *Nash* by going to touch the paperboy and in *Toothill* by trying to enter the building. However, in both cases the courts felt they had embarked on the crime proper and moved into execution, therefore satisfying the *actus reus*.

However, there are still a number of problems associated with the *actus reus* of attempts.

One of the main problems has been what exactly is meant by 'more than merely preparatory'? Since there is no definition in the Act, each court can, and has, given different interpretations of the phrase. This suggests that the statement is not accurate and the law has not developed accurately as there is still some confusion. This was seen in *Boyle and Boyle* as discussed above. However, there is an argument that the law has developed since cases like *Geddes* and *Gullefer* have simply helped juries to decide what the *actus reus* is and can be interpreted as being. Ultimately the decision is left to the jury. However, this creates two problems – firstly no two juries are the same and may come to different decisions in similar cases. Secondly, the courts are therefore stating what the law is which is not democratic. The Act has the 'definition' of the *actus reus* and it should therefore simply be left to the jury to decide without further assistance. Further clarification is needed by Parliament.

In the Law Commission report of 2007 a number of suggestions were made for the law on attempts, such as adding omissions and rebranding the law on attempts into two offences – criminal preparation and attempts itself. However, this simply remains a report and has not been acted upon by Parliament.

In conclusion, this statement does accurately reflect the law on the *actus reus* of attempts. While there was confusion before 1981 as to which common law test was to be used, the 1981 Act has allowed a greater adherence to one definition. It is arguable that the definition was vague but subsequent cases have assisted in the understanding of the phrase. Nevertheless, whether Parliament intended the courts to provide further assistance such as in *Geddes* and *Jones* remains uncertain.

Exam comment

This is a wide-ranging and accurate candidate response which is well deserving of a high grade. They clearly structure their response to the question by looking at where the law was before 1981 and how the law has developed after that date.

AO1 – the candidate continuously provides well developed explanations of the *actus reus* of attempts. There are well developed definitions of the *actus reus* of attempts and there are 11 cases discussed by the candidate. Of these cases, all bar one case (*Widdowson*) are developed in some way by either stating the facts or explaining how important the decision was on the law. Many of the cases go beyond those used in the source material, showing the candidate's own independent study.

AO2 – the candidate provides a sophisticated level of evaluation on the *actus reus* and is very focused on the quote throughout. The AO2 has an excellent ability to balance between the analytical comment on how the law has, or hasn't, developed and that required by the quote.

Mid-level response

The issues surrounding whether or not the defendant moved from the 'realm of preparation and planning into the area of execution or implementation' (Source 2, lines 16–17) has caused problems throughout the law, due to the difficulty in deciding when this has happened. It can be argued that this statement from *Geddes* has both restricted and developed the law.

Previous to the Criminal Attempts Act 1981 there were various tests used to decide whether D had committed an attempted crime (Source 1, lines 5–8). These tests included the last act and proximity tests (*Eagleton*). They were problematic as it was hard to determine whether or not an attempt had been committed and did not provide much discretion or flexibility in the law. It can thus be found that the statement from *Geddes* developed the law on *actus reus* of attempts considerably as it provided a basis upon which the jury could begin their decision-making and helped to clarify what is meant by 'more than merely preparatory' – Source 1, lines 10–13. In *Geddes* D was found in some toilets with a rope and a knife and was clearly trying to kidnap a young boy. But he was found not guilty because he hadn't done enough for the attempted crime. He had not done an act which was 'more than merely preparatory'.

The law on the *actus reus* also developed through *Gullefer* which stated that an attempt began when D 'embarked on the crime proper' (Source 1, line 29). The statement from *Geddes* and *Gullefer* both gave some help to the jury in deciding when an attempt had begun and they can be found to have developed the law on attempts concerning the *actus reus*.

It can also be argued that the statement given in *Geddes* has not developed the law, leaving problems for the police. It is not clear for them when they should intervene to get a balance between public protection and getting a conviction. What the police may believe is an act of execution the jury or judge may not. Furthermore, a policeman could intervene too late and run the risk of causing harm to the public because it wasn't known when the right time was to intervene.

The case of *Geddes* seems to show the courts following the law precisely rather than looking to protect the public. In such cases people with blatant intent to commit a crime can escape conviction. However, the previous laws also raised the same problems.

The Law Commission felt in 2007 that this type of situation was not good. They proposed there should be two separate crimes for 'preparation' and that of attempt itself. This would mean that in the case of *Geddes* they wouldn't have escaped conviction and this would have protected the public.

The statement from Bingham LJ can be found to have developed the law though, as it did help clarify what was meant by 'more than merely preparatory' and what constitutes the *actus reus*. There are, however, great inconsistencies throughout the cases concerning attempts, where some would argue a conviction should be gained from cases such as *Campbell* and *Gullefer*.

It has been decided that the judge should decide if there is enough evidence to convict and that it shouldn't be up to unqualified juries to do this task for them.

In conclusion the statement from Bingham LJ has developed the law, providing a definition of what is meant by more than merely preparatory, but it can reflect that it doesn't develop the law on the *actus reus* of attempted crimes due to the problems raised above.

Exam comment

This candidate begins by setting the scene on *actus reus* of attempts. However, they simply reword the question which uses up valuable time. This student clearly understands the topic area but their level of detail and analysis prevents them from achieving higher marks. Their points are too brief and they do not expand using enough detail.

AO1 – the candidate provides adequate explanations together with adequate definitions of the *actus reus*.

There are four cases used, but only two of these could be described as well developed – *Gullefer* and *Geddes*. The other two cases are simply named.

AO2 – there is adequate evaluation of the law. Most of the candidate's response makes some comment but the comments are basic and not developed. There are some references to the quote, but again, the analysis is mechanically applied where the candidate has discussed the issue.

Student activity

Identify three things that this candidate could have done to improve their response for both AO1 and AO2.

Lower-level response

The statement: 'Had [the defendant] moved from the realm of ... preparation and planning into the area of execution or implementation?', Source 2, lines 16–17 reflects how hard it is to find if a person had done an act which is more than merely preparatory.

There were many old common law tests which were not liked by the courts. But they are still used today after the Act was passed in 1981.

The law has been decided using many cases in the courts. There are lots of cases which have developed the law but none have been particularly helpful.

Campbell has tried to develop the law of attempts by replacing the old common law tests with 'the D embarked on the crime proper' and actually tried to commit the full offence. However, it is still difficult for a jury to decide whether the act is more than merely preparatory. In a decided case the court said the last act is not the same as going beyond more than merely preparatory.

In *Campbell* this has outlined the problems between crime intervention and getting enough evidence for a conviction. It can be argued that this puts the public in danger as in *Campbell* if the imitation pistol had been real and he had entered the post office the public and staff would have been in serious danger of their lives.

In conclusion the law on attempts is vague. The Law Commission has proposed new changes but these have not been used yet.

Exam comment

This response is clearly limited in its explanation and analysis of the *actus reus*. The candidate begins by rewriting the question, which wastes time.

AO1 – there is very limited/limited explanation and definitions of the *actus reus*. Only one case is discussed in which what the candidate says is not necessarily accurate, but it does provide some definition of the law.

AO2 – the candidate has provided some analysis of the law but as their AO1 is very limited they are unable to comment more thoroughly. Their main analytical point is that of public protection which is not explained well.

Student activity

Identify five things that this candidate could have done to improve their response for both AO1 and AO2.

G154 Question 3

Revised ☐

Consider whether or not a conviction for an attempted crime is possible in each of the following situations:

a) **Latifah is out with her friends but is stopped from entering a pub by Douglas, a door supervisor. Angered by this, Latifah tries to smash a beer bottle she is carrying over Douglas' head. As she takes a swing at him, Douglas ducks to avoid the bottle and Latifah misses him. (10 marks)**

b) **Edward is in debt and decides to steal some money from the local bank. He goes to the bank armed with an imitation gun. However, when Edward gets to the bank he finds the door to the bank locked. He realises that it is closed because it is Saturday and the bank does not open on that day. (10 marks)**

c) **Jill decides that she is going to break into her neighbour Adil's house in order to steal his television, which she knows is in Adil's living room. She opens Adil's garden gate where she is startled to find his large dog, which begins to bark at her. Frightened by this, she leaves the garden and shuts the gate behind her. (10 marks)**

Higher-level response

For a)

First it needs to be considered whether Latifah's actions are 'more than merely preparatory' under section 1(1) of the Criminal Attempts Act 1981. The fact that she has actually gone on to swing the bottle at Douglas would strongly suggest her actions are more than merely preparatory. In regards to the *actus reus*, the courts would look at whether the preparatory acts had come to an end and she had embarked on the crime proper. Raising the bottle could be seen as preparatory.

Also the *Geddes* test would be applied as explained in Source 2, lines 15–17. The defendant was found in the boys' toilet of a school with a rucksack containing tape, a knife and rope. He ran away before approaching any pupils when he was seen. From this case the courts created a question for the jury of whether the defendant had moved from planning and preparation to execution and implementation.

In regards to *mens rea* the courts would refer to the *Mohan* case which defined intention. The court would look at whether Latifah made a decision 'to bring about, in so far as it lies within the accused power, the commission of the offence which it is alleged the accused attempted to commit no matter whether the accused desired that consequence or not'.

Also section 1(1) of the CAA81 says the prosecution must prove that Latifah did the act with intention to commit the offence. It is likely that Latifah has the required *actus reus* because the preparatory act would be seen when she raises the bottle and swings it at Douglas. Also by swinging the bottle at Douglas, this shows that she has moved from planning and preparation – when she raises the bottle – into the stage of execution and implementation by actually swinging the bottle at Douglas.

It is likely that the *mens rea* of intention is demonstrated by Latifah when she swings the bottle, as she has made the decision to bring about hitting Douglas with the bottle and had intent to hurt or injure him because she is angry at him.

To conclude, Latifah will be guilty of an attempted crime.

Exam comment

This is an excellent response. Since a Question 3 response requires the candidate to state the law and blend this with the actual scenario, this is clearly the tactic this candidate has gone for with detail and accuracy.

The candidate begins by explaining the law on the *actus reus* and applying each part of the definition to the scenario. Not only do they decide the act of swinging the bottle was an attempt and explain why, they also consider which act was merely preparatory.

When the candidate discusses the *mens rea* of the offence this is done thoroughly by naming a case (*Mohan*), stating what the definition is, and then finally applying this to the facts.

A specific, accurate conclusion is provided at the end.

For b)

The *actus reus* of attempts is found under s1(1) of the CAA81 and the definition of the offence can be found in Source 1, lines 10–13. The *Geddes* test can also be used to define the AR of attempts as being has the defendant moved from planning and preparation into execution and implementation?

Edward's act of going to the bank (and going up to the bank) will probably be an act of mere preparation since in *Campbell* the court decided that simply approaching the post office door was not more than merely preparatory. However, when Edward gets to the door and finds it locked then this will be deemed more than merely preparatory since there was nothing more that he could have done except enter the bank if this was possible. This put him at a stage closer than when *Campbell* was arrested. Therefore, like in *Jones*, Edward's act of getting to the bank placed him in the position of execution and implementation, satisfying the *actus reus* of attempts. But because the bank was closed it was impossible for him to enter.

Edward clearly wanted to rob the bank since it was his plan and decision to bring about, in so far as it lies within his powers to rob the bank as defined in *Mohan*. Clearly going to the bank with an imitation gun would prove that he wanted to rob the bank.

However, Edward could try to argue that the crime was impossible since it was a Saturday and the bank was therefore closed. However, s(2) CAA81 (see Source 6, lines 9–10) would allow a conviction for attempting the impossible which was confirmed in *Shivpuri* (see Source 6, lines 14–17 for the facts), where he was found guilty of attempting the impossible. This decision would apply to Edward.

Therefore, since the *actus reus* and *mens rea* are present for a charge of convicted robbery, and even though it was impossible to commit, Edward would be convicted with attempted robbery.

Exam comment

This response, although not detailed in every area, does provide an excellent answer. This candidate's discussion on the *actus reus* is thorough, defining it and applying it to the scenario. The candidate looks at both sides of the dividing line and explains which acts are not attempt and which acts are, in their opinion, an attempt. This is nicely blended with relevant cases.

The discussion of the *mens rea* is fine. However, there is no mention of the word 'intent' and no definition.

What the candidate does do well is apply what they don't say to the scenario.

The final piece of analysis is that they clearly identify the issue of impossibility. The candidate states the law and applies it to the situation.

The final mark is gained in providing an accurate, specific conclusion.

Identify three things that this candidate could have done to improve their response for both AO1 and AO2.

For c)

First it must be considered whether Jill's actions are 'more than merely preparatory' under s1(1) of the Criminal Attempts Act 1981. Jill only gets as far as opening Adil's gate before running away. It is likely that her acts are just preparatory as she was not in a position to be more than merely preparatory as she still had time to turn away and had not passed the point of beginning the implementation of her plan. She was frightened by the dog so ran away.

In terms of *actus reus*, the *Geddes* test would be applied. It is unlikely Jill's acts had moved from planning to implementation. For it to be seen as implementation, Jill would have to have got much further than the gate – probably she would have to have entered the house and certainly it would have been an attempt if she had entered the living room. In *Campbell* the defendant was found not guilty of attempted robbery when he approached a post office. The court said he had time to change his mind and walk away. Jill could have done the same as she approached the house.

In regard to the *mens rea*, under s1(1) it would be likely that Jill satisfies the *mens rea* of intention to commit theft or burglary as she clearly intended to steal the TV. In *Moloney* this was defined as a defendant wanting the true desire to bring about the consequence. Jill clearly had a true desire to bring about the consequence of appropriating Adil's TV.

Therefore, in conclusion, as the *actus reus* is not satisfied, Jill would not be guilty of an attempted offence.

Exam comment

This is a thorough response as the candidate looks at all the relevant parts of the offence in detail. They begin by defining the *actus reus* and applying it to the situation. They look at why they believe it to be mere preparation as the defendant only gets as far as the gate, and then state what she would have to have done in order for the situation to have moved into becoming an attempt.

The *mens rea* discussion is excellent since it names a relevant case, defines it, and accurately applies it to this situation.

Given this thorough discussion on attempts, the candidate makes an accurate and specific conclusion.

Student activity

Identify three things that this candidate could have done to improve their response for both AO1 and AO2.

Mid-level response

For a)

The definition of the Criminal Attempts Act can be found in Source 1, lines 10–13: 'If with intent to commit an offence to which this section applies, a person does an act which is more than merely preparatory to the commission of the offence, he is guilty of attempting to commit the offence'.

Latifah is stopped from entering a pub by Douglas and Latifah is angry about this. We are not told why Douglas stops her but it may be because she is wearing the wrong type of clothes like trainers or something similar. The attempt might be a possible attempted GBH which is defined in *Smith* as an intent to do really serious harm. It would be difficult to know how much damage a bottle would have caused Douglas if it had hit him over the head.

Latifah has clear intent as seen in *Whybrow*. She is angry and has acted in this way. The *actus reus* is also apparent since she has tried to hurt him. Intent is defined under *Mohan* as a decision to bring about in so far as it lies within the defendant's power. Latifah did this.

It would be up to the prosecution to decide what charge would be brought against Latifah. However, it carries the minimum sentence of all the non-fatal offences which is five years.

Overall, perhaps Latifah would be guilty of an attempt. Essentially this is a matter for the jury to decide. Perhaps Latifah could bring the defence of intoxication as she had been drinking heavily that day.

Exam comment

This response clearly identifies the *actus reus* of attempts and applies it to the scenario. However, the candidate rephrases the question and introduces some hypothetical situations which the question does not require. They then define the *actus reus* of the full offence which is not required in this case and again discuss a hypothetical situation if the victim had actually been hit.

When it comes to the discussion on the *mens rea*, the candidate simply states a case with no definition and therefore does not apply this to the situation. Instead, they say Latifah is angry.

In the conclusion the candidate discusses what sentence could be given to the defendant which is irrelevant. They also fail to make a specific conclusion by using the word 'perhaps', which is too vague.

Student activity

Identify three things that this candidate could have done to improve their response for both AO1 and AO2.

For b)

The law on criminal attempts is defined in Source 1, lines 10–14. The scenario is concerned with the *actus reus* of attempts and as to whether the defendant has embarked on the crime proper. As Edward is in debt and decides to steal money from the bank he has the intention.

However, the question is whether he has done acts considered more than merely preparatory. Getting the imitation gun would only be preparatory, as would arriving outside the bank.

As it is closed there is no way he can rob the bank. For this offence there must be violence and therefore Edward is not at the attempt stage.

However, it is possible that the jury will decide that this is not an attempt as this is similar to *Campbell* in which the defendant was not convicted.

Exam comment

The response begins by using an accurate and relevant source reference, saving the candidate time in writing out the definition. However, the acceptable brevity of this approach is continued, since the rest of the response, while covering the salient points, fails to expand beyond a brief discussion on each point.

There is some further definition on the *actus reus* and *mens rea* but no real detail. However, the candidate sees the similarity between this case and that of *Campbell* and follows the decision in *Campbell* to mean the same here. Where *Campbell* had been some distance away from the post office, the defendant in this scenario had actually arrived at the door and discovered it closed.

Nevertheless, there is a fair description of being mere preparation. The student sees the issue of the bank being closed but misses the likelihood of impossibility.

The conclusion is therefore inaccurate. While the candidate follows the thought process behind the decision in *Campbell*, they do not see the differences.

Student activity

Identify three things that this candidate could have done to improve their response for both AO1 and AO2.

For c)

The *actus reus* of attempts under s1(1) CAA81 can be found in the source, along with the *Geddes* test.

Jill's actions are not more than merely preparatory as she has not moved from planning and preparation to implementation. Therefore, she doesn't meet this requirement as she is not at the house. In order to meet this criteria she must have at least gone to the house.

The *mens rea* of attempts is intent to commit the substantive offence. Jill clearly has intention as she intends to go to Adil's house and steal the TV from his front room. Therefore, she satisfies the MR of attempts (*Mohan*).

In the case of *Geddes* D was found in the toilets of a school with rope, tape and a knife. He was found not guilty.

Since Jill fails to meet the AR of attempts she is unlikely to be found guilty.

Exam comment

This response begins with a vague source reference and cannot be fully credited since it contains no specific source or line numbers. The candidate does provide a common law interpretation from *Geddes* in the second paragraph but does not fully apply it to the scenario. The candidate rejects the attempted offence, but again the application as to why is vague.

The *mens rea* is discussed and the candidate explains why they think the defendant has the *mens rea*. There is no definition even though a case name is used.

The conclusion provided is not specific and therefore cannot be credited.

Student activity

Identify three things this candidate could have done to improve their response for both AO1 and AO2.

Lower-level response

For a)

Latifah could be convicted with attempted GBH. This is where a person cuts the skin but doesn't actually do it. This is under the Act in the source. When she went to the pub and was refused entry she was angry and took a swing at the doorman with the bottle. She went past the stage of mere preparation and intended to hit Douglas. She is guilty of an attempted crime.

Exam comment

The candidate begins with a conclusion. However, the conclusion is vague since they use the word 'could'. This is not specific enough. They then define part of the *actus reus* of a full offence which is not necessary here. Since the topic is on attempts, the expectation is that they define and apply the definition of attempts.

The candidate does refer to the source, but gives no source number or line numbers. There is some effort to apply the definition to the scenario but this is too brief and mechanical.

The final conclusion is specific and accurate.

Student activity

Identify five things that this candidate could have done to improve their response for both AO1 and AO2.

For b)

Edward can be convicted with attempted robbery as he did get past the point of mere preparation. When he got to the door he realised that it was Saturday and the bank doesn't open on that day. This would make the crime impossible. It may be that as he didn't put fear into anyone it can't be robbery. But this will not stop it being an attempt. Although Edward intended to rob the bank he was at the more than merely preparatory stage.

Exam comment

This response begins with a conclusion which is correct. The candidate explains, however very briefly, why this is so. They spot the further issue of impossibility and explain why this is so.

The candidate then discusses vaguely the definition of the full crime, which is not necessary here. The answer ends with a brief mention of the *mens rea* and why it is an attempt. The response is brief and had the candidate expanded on all of the points made with further application and definition, the answer would have been much better.

Student activity

Identify five things that this candidate could have done to improve their response for both AO1 and AO2.

For c)

Jill didn't go past the point of preparation so would not be convicted with an attempted crime. Although she did intend to steal (Mohan) she didn't go past the point of wanting to do something but didn't. She is not more than merely preparatory because in order to do this she would have had to go to the house at least. Opening the garden gate is trespassing on her neighbour's property.

Exam comment

This response is vague. The candidate begins with an accurate conclusion. They then mention the *mens rea* stating an accurate case, but are unable to define this and do not apply this to the scenario.

The candidate mentions the *actus reus* of attempts and explains why they think the defendant is not at that stage.

The final sentence seems to have little, if any, relevance, although it could have been developed into a valid point.

Student activity

Identify five things that this candidate could have done to improve their response for both AO1 and AO2.

Answers

Chapter 1

OMISSIONS

Check your understanding

1 Voluntary act, 'being there', result crime.

2 Any of s6 Road Traffic Act 1988, s170 Road Traffic Act 1988, s1 Children and Young Persons Act 1933, s5 Domestic Violence, Crime and Victims Act 2004.

3 Contractual duty applies to anyone who has a job whilst one resulting from an official position is an extension to this duty but only applies to those who have special jobs such as the police and members of the emergency services.

4 The law is fair to an extent as people should take responsibility for what they do but it becomes unfair if they do not know exactly what they are letting themselves in for and they may not be able to fulfil the duty they have assumed.

5 It might mean a lot of people commit offences, someone required to help might make things worse and the photographers in the Princess Diana case suggest it does not necessarily improve behaviour.

Now test yourself

1 Look at the following chart and note down the reason why there is a duty in each case. Tip: some cases are covered by more than one duty.

Case	Duty
Pittwood (1902)	Contract
Dytham (1979)	Public office
Instan (1893)	Reliance/relationship
Gibbins and Proctor (1918)	Relationship
Stone and Dobinson (1977)	Reliance/relationship
Evans (2009)	Dangerous situation/relationship
Miller (1983)	Dangerous situation
Santana-Bermudez (2003)	Dangerous situation
Adomako (1995)	Contract

2 Use the tables on pages 10 and 11 to check your answers.

CAUSATION

Check your understanding

6 It shows that there is a limit to the protection offered to doctors – 'palpably wrong' test.

7 The victim's own act, the act of a third party or something which is natural but unpredictable.

8 It means that without the defendant's act the harm would not have occurred. Good as there is always someone responsible but bad as liability is not always allocated justly or correctly.

9 The case is important as it shows that a victim can break the chain by self-injection but raises difficult issues of personal responsibility against needing to protect the vulnerable.

10 It makes it easier to establish liability. It can be very unfair on the defendant.

Now test yourself

3 Use the tables on pages 14 and 15 to check your answers.

Chapter 2

MENS REA

Intention

Check your understanding

1 Doing everything to achieve a consequence and really wanting it to happen.

2 The defendant does not necessarily intend the consequence to happen but knows that pretty much nothing else will be the result.

3 It changed the test to being subjective and it said that foresight was only evidence of intention and had to be considered along with everything else.

4 Probability. This was important as it is the level of the consequence occurring that links to blame and therefore justifies punishment.

5 It is simpler and clearer, allowing them to reach verdicts with greater confidence. 90% or over.

Now test yourself

1 Use the table on page 18 to check your answers.

Recklessness

Check your understanding

6 The defendant sees the risk and decides to take it – *Lidar (2000)*.

7 The defendant does not see a risk obvious to the reasonable man – *Caldwell (1982)*.

8 Driving without due care and attention or gross negligence manslaughter.

9 Coincidence allows for a momentary coming together of *actus reus and mens rea*. It allows liability to be extended.

10 Otherwise it would be easy for defendants to avoid liability for a consequence to an unintended person.

Now test yourself

2 For each of the following scenarios decide whether there is likely to be an offence, based on the existence of *mens rea*, and give a brief justification for your answer.

a) Offence based on subjective recklessness as goes to house with loaded gun.

b) Offence based on objective recklessness and made worse as P is drunk.

c) Offence based on coincidence.

d) Offence based on transferred malice.

Chapter 3

STRICT LIABILITY

Check your understanding

1 3500.

2 No *mens rea* is needed for at least one element of the *actus reus*. Example: selling a lottery ticket to a person under age.

3 No *mens rea* is needed and the *actus reus* need not be voluntary. Example: being drunk on a public highway.

4 It sets out the general principles which dictate how this area of law works.

5 A more minor offence. They are supposed to lead to better behaviour and drive up standards but this is not always the result in the case of large companies who can afford to take risks.

Now test yourself

1 Look at the following chart and decide if a strict liability offence has been committed by putting a tick in the correct column.

Act	Strict liability offence occurs	Strict liability offence does not occur
Sue gives a rabbit to Mark. Mark cooks the rabbit and eats it. Mark is very ill.		✓
Sue is an architect who designs an eco-friendly house for a client, Dan. Dan builds the house but takes some short cuts to save money. Dan sells the house to Freda. Freda has lived in the house for a week when the roof falls in.	✓	

(Continued)

(Continued)

Act	Strict liability offence occurs	Strict liability offence does not occur
Stefan is a barman. Jude wants to buy a drink and Stefan asks to see proof of his age. Jude shows Stefan an ID card which says he is 19. In fact Jude is 15 but looks older. Stefan sells Jude a pint of lager.	✓	
Kevin has a business which takes water from the local river and pumps it back into the river when the steel his factory is making has been processed. Fred is employed to keep the filters clean but goes on holiday for two weeks without telling Kevin. The filters are not cleaned and toxins leak into the river, killing fish and some swans.	✓	
Kevin sacks Fred and employs Guy to clean the filters. One night vandals break in and tip some of the chemicals used to process the steel into the river, killing fish and some swans.	✓	
Kevin's factory is on a big industrial estate near an airport. A terrorist plants a bomb on the estate intending to blow up the airport. The blast explodes some of the chemical containers Kevin is storing and chemicals go into the river, killing fish and several swans.		✓
Buy-Wise supermarket is supplied with pork pies by HappyPies. Harry buys a pie and suffers food poisoning.	✓	

2 Use the chart on pages 25–27 to check your answers.

Chapter 4

ATTEMPT

Check your understanding

1 s1(1).

2 An act which is more than merely preparatory to the full offence.

3 Intention.

4 s1(2) and s1(3) – factual and legal.

5 2007.

Now test yourself

1 & 2 Refer back to the charts on pages 32 and 33 to check your answers.

3 **i)** Yes – B has intention to kill and has done all he can.

    ii) No – S does not have enough MR as she 'hopes' for money.

    iii) Yes – R has intention, no matter that crime is impossible.

    iv) Yes – W has done enough to be 'a crime proper'.

Chapter 5

MURDER AND DEFENCES

Check your understanding

1 s55.

2 A fear of serious violence or a thing or things done or said (or both) which constitutes circumstances of an extremely grave character and causes the defendant to have a justifiable sense of being seriously wronged.

3 There must be an abnormality of mental functioning which causes substantial impairment and is an explanation for conduct.

4 It has been abolished and so there is a chance for a fresh start.

5 Unless it is ADS there has to be substantial impairment from an abnormality of mind without the effect of intoxication.

Now test yourself

1 Use the table on page 43 to check your answers.

Chapter 6

INVOLUNTARY MANSLAUGHTER

Check your understanding

1 *Lidar* (2000).

2 It makes it clear that there was no need to foresee harm as long as there was *mens rea* for the act in unlawful act manslaughter.

3 It is circular in that criminality is decided by an act being gross negligence and gross negligence is determined by the act being criminal.

4 It is objective which goes against the subjective test used elsewhere.

5 It is a relatively common offence, juries need to be sure to deliver consistency and blame needs to be allocated appropriately.

Now test yourself

1 Look at the following chart and decide what type of manslaughter charge is most likely.

Act	Manslaughter type
Andreas offers to care for his ageing grandmother who is confined to bed. She is not always grateful for the things Andreas does for her and after an argument he takes her no food for three days. The next time Andreas goes into his grandmother's room she has died.	Gross negligence
Brenda is a teacher. She takes some children on a hike but does not check the route beforehand. The hike takes the children along steep cliffs. Instead of turning back Brenda tells the children to keep walking. A child falls off the cliff and is killed.	Gross negligence
Christine is a chef and she gets into an argument with Daphne, another chef, whom Christine accuses of being an alcoholic. Christine waves a knife at Daphne, who has been drinking. Daphne runs towards Christine but cannot keep her balance because she is drunk. She falls into Christine and on to the knife Christine is holding. Daphne dies.	Unlawful act
Edward is a police officer on duty in the city centre on a Saturday night. He sees a fight break out in which a man slashes a girl with a bottle. Edward sees the girl fall to the floor but he gets into his patrol car and drives off. The girl dies.	Gross negligence
Frank has been suspended from school and he is very angry with the headmaster. He decides to start a fire at the school. He throws a petrol bomb through a window and runs off. The school caretaker sees the flames and tries to fight the blaze but dies from smoke inhalation.	Unlawful act

2 Use the tables on pages 46–48 to check your answers.

Chapter 7

NON–FATAL OFFENCES AGAINST THE PERSON

Check your understanding

1 Putting a person in fear of immediate and unlawful personal harm.

2 Hostile touching.

3 Intention or subjective recklessness for the initial unlawful act.

4 A wound must break all the layers of the skin but GBH can be physical, internal or psychiatric.

5 Intention or subjective recklessness for the initial unlawful act and foresight of some harm although not necessarily the serious harm that results.

Now test yourself

1 Look at the following chart and decide on the most appropriate non-fatal offence against the person in each of the following situations.

Act	Non–fatal offence
Sue has fallen out with her neighbour, Paul. Sue goes to Paul's house with a knife in her pocket and when he opens the door she stabs him in the stomach.	s18
Richard is drunk in a city park. A policeman tries to arrest Richard and Richard head butts the policeman, breaking his nose.	s47
Kate is washing up when she sees a stranger, Colin, standing in her garden and staring through the window at her.	Assault
Dave is walking his dog when Keith comes past on his mountain bike. Keith pushes Dave, who falls over grazes his knee.	Battery
Albert has just been beaten by Fred in a local gardening competition to grow the biggest marrow. Albert waves his spade at Fred who trips and Albert's spade cuts Fred's head very badly.	s20

2 Use the tables on pages 53–54 and 56–57 to check your answers.

CONSENT

Check your understanding

6 People have a right to make decisions about what happens to them.

7 The offences were based on degradation and cruelty which was felt to be unacceptable despite consent and harm which did not require medical treatment.

8 It is allowed as long as it occurs within the rules of a properly conducted sport.

9 Branding was held to be like tattooing and so prosecution was not in the public interest.

10 It was the first time transmission of a disease led to conviction for a non-fatal offence.

Now test yourself

4 Use the table on pages 59–60 to check your answers.

Chapter 8

INSANITY

Check your understanding

1 1843 – outdated as medical science has changed.

2 1991 – broadened although compulsory detention still needed for murder.

3 As a mental disorder.

4 It creates a very broad definition for a disease of the mind which arguably does not catch the right people.

5 It is fair because he had killed his wife and the way in which he did so suggests he knew exactly what he was doing, especially in view of what he said to the police. It is unfair because W was ill as he had a mental condition based on living with a wife who was mentally ill for many years. Also when he committed the offence the death penalty still existed for murder and diminished responsibility had not been created.

AUTOMATISM

Check your understanding

6 D has no control over actions and no *mens rea* due to an external factor.

7 Some kinds of stress can give rise to automatism.

8 Automatism may be a defence if intoxication is linked to a specific intent offence but not if the crime is one of basic intent.

9 It means that automatism will not work if there is some voluntary control left – this is often the case in driving offences.

10 Sleepwalking would come within automatism.

Now test yourself

1 Look at the following chart and decide on the most appropriate defence in each of the situations described.

Act	Insanity or automatism
Sanjay asks Misha to go out with him. She refuses so he asks again. She refuses again. Sanjay sees Misha in the street with another boy and runs up to her, hitting her with a cricket bat he is carrying shouting, 'If I can't have you, neither can he!'	Insanity
Trevor is a teacher and a diabetic. He is late for class and does not have time to take his insulin. During the class Trevor grabs Carly by the throat and she faints. Trevor says he can remember nothing.	Insanity

(Continued)

(Continued)

Act	Insanity or automatism
Vincent is a diabetic and he has taken his insulin but did not have time for lunch. Trevor drives home and crashes into a parked car. He recalls nothing but calls the police the next morning when he sees that his car has been damaged by the crash.	Insanity if he has been reckless in not eating
Xavier's sister has been prescribed tranquilisers for her depression. Xavier has had a big argument with his mother and he is so angry he takes some of his sister's tranquilisers to help him calm down. The tranquilisers make Xavier hyperactive and he smashes two windows and a coffee table before falling asleep.	Automatism
Benedict invites a friend to watch a film with him. Benedict attacks his friend and says he was sleepwalking.	Insanity

2 Use the tables on pages 63 and 65 to check your answers.

Chapter 9

DURESS AND NECESSITY

Check your understanding

1 Was the defendant compelled to act because he reasonably believed he had good reason to fear death or serious injury? (subjective) and would a sober person of reasonable firmness, sharing the same characteristics as the defendant, have acted in the same way? (objective with a subjective element)

2 It seems harsh that the son had no defence when he felt he had to act because he was so scared of his father.

3 It could become available for murder and it could be a partial defence.

4 It seems to say that necessity is available for murder.

5 It is open to inconsistency and if there is a defence the law should be open and admit that this is the case.

Now test yourself

1 Use the tables on pages 70–71 and 72 to check your answers.

Chapter 10

INTOXICATION

Check your understanding

1 It is no defence as it would be an easy excuse for criminality.

2 It makes it clear that recklessness in becoming voluntarily intoxicated provides the *mens rea* for the offence committed.

3 It creates a particular defence but only to criminal damage.

4 This means that there can be a conviction for a lesser included offence, such as murder down to manslaughter, but it is problematic in theft which is a common offence and has no fall-back offence.

5 It is important as it makes it clear that a mistake as to the need for force in self-defence will not succeed if it is because of intoxication.

SELF-DEFENCE

Check your understanding

6 It said there is no duty to retreat.

7 This is likely to result in the defence being unavailable.

8 The mistake is to be assessed from the defendant's perspective and if it is reasonable from that perspective.

9 Criminal Justice and Immigration Act 2008.

10 It should be a defence because it makes a person act in a way they would not normally do. It can be hard for juries to put themselves in the shoes of the defendant and there is pressure on the jury as the defence is all or nothing.

Now test yourself

1 Look at the following chart, decide on the most appropriate defence in each of the following situations and comment on whether the defence is likely to be successful.

	Intoxication or self-defence	Reasoning
Yuri wants to kills his father so he can inherit his money. Yuri drinks a bottle of vodka and then stabs his father with a knife.	Intoxication	No defence as this is Dutch courage
Eric has been on a night out and climbs into the house he rents by breaking a small window as the landlord has told him this is OK. When Eric gets inside he realises he has broken into the house next door.	Intoxication	Defence under s5 CDA 1971
Anya has been to a party to celebrate her new job. She drinks only orange juice but is stopped by the police after she is seen driving the wrong way round a roundabout and breathalysed. Anya is over the limit because her friends put vodka in her orange juice.	Intoxication	May be a defence of involuntary intoxication if Anya can show she did not feel intoxicated and had no *mens rea*

(Continued)

(Continued)

	Intoxication or self-defence	Reasoning
Rupert has been drinking all day to celebrate his A Level results. As he is going home Rupert is approached by a man. The man is going to ask Rupert for money but Rupert thinks he is about to be attacked and punches the man so hard his nose is broken.	Intoxication/ self-defence	Unlikely to be a defence as force used is excessive and mistake induced by voluntary intoxication
Sasha is a heroin addict. Her dealer demands more money for the heroin he sells her. Sasha pays the dealer but she is so angry she follows him down the street and hits him from behind with a brick. The dealer dies.	Intoxication	Likely to be no defence unless intoxication has become involuntary

2 Use the tables on pages 77 and 79 to check your answers.

Chapter 11

THEFT

Check your understanding

1 Dishonest appropriation of property belonging to another with the intention to permanently deprive the other of it.

2 Appropriation is any interference with any right of the owner and it can occur with consent.

3 s5(3) is when there is an obligation to use property in a particular way and s5(4) is when property is received by mistake but there is a legal obligation to restore it.

4 Is the defendant dishonest by the standards of the reasonable man and does the defendant realise they are dishonest by those standards? It is used when s2 and common sense are insufficient and it is important because dishonesty is now the key discriminator in theft.

5 There is no need to permanently deprive and the assessment of how much value has to be lost is not always clear.

Now test yourself

1 Fill in the details in the table below to test your knowledge.

Act	Theft or no theft?	Relevant Theft Act section
Ann is in a shop and picks up a lipstick. She slips it into her pocket thinking she will pay if she is challenged. Ann leaves the shop without paying for the lipstick.	Theft	3, 2

(Continued)

(Continued)

Act	Theft or no theft?	Relevant Theft Act section
Brendan has had a row with this girlfriend. He sees some daffodils growing in a nearby park and picks them to give to his girlfriend as a peace offering.	Theft	4
Callum goes to a restaurant with some friends. He leaves his coat behind. Next week he goes to the same restaurant and as it is raining he takes a coat from the restaurant. Unknown to Callum he has taken his own coat.	Theft	5
Derek is in the supermarket. He pays with a £10 note but is given change for a £20 note. Derek realises he has too much money the next morning and the supermarket is six miles away.	No theft – there is too much time and distance for liability	5(4)
Ellen works in a busy company office. She is short of money and takes company paper and pens home for her children to use at school.	Theft	2
Frank is a student who needs to photocopy a large document for an assignment. He borrows his flatmate's photocopy card, thinking his flatmate will not mind, to photocopy the document and then puts it back, although the card is out of credit when his flatmate tries to use it.	Theft	6

2 Use the tables on pages 84–86 to check your answers.

Chapter 12

ROBBERY AND BURGLARY

Check your understanding

1 Theft accompanied by force or the threat of force used before or at the time of stealing and in order to steal.

2 Nothing was actually taken and relies on completion of theft being very early.

3 Entry of a building or part of a building as a trespasser with the intention to steal, inflict GBH or do unlawful damage.

4 s9(1)(b) differs as there need only be intention to enter as a trespasser and the ulterior offences are theft, attempted theft, infliction of GBH or attempted infliction of GBH.

5 It says that entry in burglary need not even be effective.

Now test yourself

1 For each of the following scenarios decide whether an offence of robbery or burglary has been committed, giving reasons for your answer.

Act	Offence or no offence?
Mike walks up to Nathan and says, 'Give me £10'. Nathan hands over £10.	Probably no robbery but depends on what accompanies words
Oliver is wearing a Rolex watch. Patrick runs up to Oliver and grabs his arm, demanding that Oliver take his watch off. Oliver refuses but he drops his mobile phone and Patrick runs off with Oliver's phone.	Robbery – force has been used before theft and property taken
Quentin goes into a shop intending to get some new jeans by trying a pair on and then walking out of the shop wearing them. He tries on several pairs of jeans but none fit and he leaves the shop still wearing his old jeans.	Technically s9(1)(a) as offence complete on entry

(Continued)

(Continued)

Act	Offence or no offence?
Richard breaks into a nearby house as he knows the owner has lots of antique silver and is on holiday. Inside the house all the silver has been locked away. Richard is so angry he finds a jar of curry sauce and throws it on the white carpet in the living room.	s9(1)(a) at entry. Unlikely to be s9(1)(b) unless damage to carpet is such that it is destruction and seen as theft
Trevor is at a pop festival and sees that the girl in a nearby tent has a very expensive camera. When the girl goes to see a band Trevor reaches into the girl's tent and takes the camera.	Unlikely to be burglary as a tent is not a building

2 Use the tables on pages 90 and 91 to check your answers.